Whitney Houston

Julia Holt

Published in association with The Basic Skills Agency

Hodder & Stoughton

A MEMBER OF THE HODDER HEADLINE GROUP

Acknowledgements

Photos: pp. iv, 6, 11 © Popperfoto/Reuter, p. 14 © Jean Cummings/All Action, pp. 18, 21 © Alpha, pp. 25, 28 © Steve Finn/Alpha.

Cover photo: © Alpha.

Orders: please contact Bookpoint Ltd, 39 Milton Park, Abingdon, Oxon OX14 4TD. Telephone: (44) 01235 400414, Fax: (44) 01235 400454. Lines are open from 9.00–6.00, Monday to Saturday, with a 24 hour message answering service. Email address: orders@bookpoint.co.uk

British Library Cataloguing in Publication Data
A catalogue record for this title is available from The British Library

ISBN 0 340 71152 3

First published 1998
Impression number 10 9 8 7 6 5 4 3 2 1
Year 2002 2001 2000 1999 1998

Typeset by Fakenham Photosetting Ltd, Fakenham, Norfolk.
Printed in Great Britain for Hodder & Stoughton Educational, a division of Hodder Headline Plc, 338 Euston Road, London NW1 3BH by Page Bros Ltd, Norwich.

Contents

1 Growing up with Music

From the moment Whitney Houston
first sang in public
it was obvious she had a great talent.

She was 11 years old
when she sang solo
at the New Hope Baptist Church.
No-one moved,
everyone stared
and at the end, everyone clapped and cried.

It is no surprise that she has talent.
She was born into a talented family.

Her mother Cissy Houston
was a successful back-up singer
and solo artist back in the 1960s and '70s.
She was the first singer
to record 'Midnight Train To Georgia'.

Whitney's cousin is Dionne Warwick.
She was world famous in the 1970s
with songs like 'I Say A Little Prayer'.

Whitney was born on 19 August 1963,
in Newark, New Jersey.

In the 1960s
Newark was a place of social unrest.
Black people took their fight for
civil rights onto the streets.
There were many riots.

Cissy and her husband John
moved out of the city.
They wanted a quiet place
to bring up their three children.
There was Whitney
and her two older brothers,
Michael and Gary.

Every week they went back to the city
to go to church.
Cissy was their Minister of Music
and Whitney sang in the choir.

Whitney grew up with music.
She said:
'Singing was so natural to me
that when I started singing,
it was almost like speaking.'

She heard gospel music in church
and rhythm and blues from Cissy's friends.
Those friends were great singers
like Gladys Knight and Aretha Franklin.
Whitney called Aretha 'Aunty Ree'.

When Whitney was small,
she wanted to be a teacher or a vet.
But by the age of ten,
she knew she had to be a singer.

After her first success
singing solo in church,
she began to practise.
She put on her mother's stage dresses
and sang along to Aunty Ree's records.

Cissy is a strong woman.
She has played an important part
in Whitney's life and her career.
She told her to work hard
and never forget her family.
She said her talent
was a gift from God.

Whitney heard her mother
sing in church many times.
Whitney said:
'It's like electricity running through you.
That's what I wanted.'

2 Schoolgirl to Superstar

Whitney was sent to a Catholic school
because Cissy said they were strict.
At home she did not wear lipstick
or high heels until her mother said so.

In the school holidays,
Whitney went on tour with her mother.
Sometimes she was given a solo spot
in one of the shows.
As she got older,
she was given more songs to sing
and so it went on.
Cissy was not only teaching her to sing
but also how to be strong
and successful in business.

Whitney grew up into a beautiful woman.
She was tall and slim just like a model.
In 1981 she was spotted in New York
by a man from a modelling agency.
Photos of her were in glossy magazines
like Cosmopolitan.

Modelling led to offers to appear on TV.
But she was in even more demand
as a singer.

One night Clive Davis,
the President of Arista Records,
heard Whitney sing on stage.
He signed her up on the spot.
She was 20 years old.

Clive knew that Whitney was going
to be a star. He said:
'She's got it.'
He was very careful
with Whitney and her talent.
They waited for two more years
until they had the perfect songs
for her first album.

The album was called simply 'Whitney Houston'.
It came out on Valentine's Day 1985.
It is the best selling first album ever
in the USA.
It stayed at No 1 in the album charts
for 14 weeks
and it was in the top 40 for a year!

One single from that first album
made Whitney a household name
in the USA and Britain.
It was called 'Saving All My Love For You'.
That single won her
two major awards in 1986.

As she started her first tour of the USA
in September 1985, she said:
'I'm being very careful with my career,
taking everything step by step.
I'm in no hurry.'

By Christmas of 1985
another single from the album was No 1
in the US charts.
It was called 'How Will I Know'.
Her third No 1 single came out in 1986.
It was 'The Greatest Love Of All'.

Whitney's first world tour was a big event.
Her brother Michael was tour manager.
She sang on a circle shaped stage
so that everyone could see her.
She sang the songs from her first album.
Her brother Gary sang some of them
with her.

Whitney was named Artist of the Year in 1986.
The next year she won
no less than five American Music Awards.
She seemed to be at the top of her career
but there was more to come.

In the summer of 1987
she sang 'I Wanna Dance With Somebody'.
It went to No 1 in the USA and the UK.
Whitney won her second Grammy
for that single, and she sang it
on her one and only Top of the Pops show.

That single was the opening track
on her second album 'Whitney'.
Her second album is more down to earth
and more fun than the first.

'Whitney' went to No 1 in the album charts
of the UK and the USA
in the first week it came out.
Whitney Houston is the first woman
ever to do this.

3 Breaking Records

By the end of 1987
she had sold 13 million albums.
She also had four more No 1 hits
from her second album.

By May 1988 she had made £30 million
from sales of her records.
She was the first artist ever
to have seven No 1 hits in a row.

Whitney had a bracelet made.
It spelled out her name
in diamonds.

In 1988,
Whitney set out on another world tour.
She played Birmingham for five nights
and Wembley for nine nights.
She came on stage in a long plain coat.
Under her coat she wore pink satin.
She looked very beautiful as she sang
'Didn't We Almost Have It All'.

Whitney on tour.

In June 1988
she was back at Wembley again.
This time she sang with many other stars
to remind the world
that Nelson Mandela was still in prison.

Whitney and Cissy sang a gospel song
'I Believe'.
She said the song was for:
'Nelson Mandela and his family,
and for all my South African
brothers and sisters'.

Whitney ended 1988
with another No 1 on both sides
of the Atlantic.
It was called 'One Moment In Time'.
She recorded it in London
for that year's Olympic Games.

By now Whitney was ready to do
something different.
She was thinking about making a film.
She looked around
but the right film wasn't there.

So she spent 1989
on tour with her friends.
They were in a group called The Winans.
They sing gospel
and Whitney was happy to be
their back-up singer.

4 Songs for Charity

Also in 1989 she set up
the Whitney Houston Foundation for Children.
It helps homeless children
and those with cancer or AIDS.

Her fans waited three and a half years
for her next album.
It came in 1990
and it was called 'I'm Your Baby Tonight'.
This album was a change for Whitney.
She moved away from
the big romantic songs
to dance music and pop songs.

It was not as successful
as her first and second albums.
Maybe her fans were not ready
for her to change.

She did have two No 1 hits in the USA
from her third album.
The songs were called:
'I'm Your Baby Tonight'
and 'All The Man That I Need'
but they were not big hits in the UK.

In 1991
she made use of her stardom
to raise money for charity.
She raised thousands in America
for victims of the Gulf War.
She also sang for the soldiers
when they came home from the Gulf.
At Wembley she sang to raise money
for the Kurdish refugees.

Whitney also did another
world tour – the third that year.
But it was not a sell out.
Some critics said the show
had too many gimmicks like fireworks.
They said it looked
like an old fashioned cabaret.
But no-one criticised her singing.

By then Whitney had spent three long years
looking for a change.
She got her change in 1992.
That year she got married and made a film.

5 A Purple Wedding

Bobby Brown had his own No 1 hit
when he was 14 years old.
He was in a boy band
called New Edition.
He went solo in 1986
and since then he has made three albums.

He has also made
a bad name for himself
with drink and drugs and women.
He already has three children
by two past girlfriends.
In two years
he was arrested four times.
He is one of the wild men of rap music.

Whitney and Bobby Brown.

Bobby and Whitney met in 1989.
They married in July 1992
at her $2.8 million house in New Jersey.
The bride and groom both wore white
and the wedding party all wore purple.
Purple is Whitney's favourite colour.

After the wedding,
there was a reception for 800 people.
Then the bride and groom flew off to France.

Whitney was already pregnant
with their first child.
Bobbi Kristina
was born in March the next year.

6 'The Bodyguard'

Whitney said in 1987:
'I'm sure that music will turn into acting.'
It did.
In 1990, Kevin Costner
asked her to be in his film,
'The Bodyguard'.
Whitney was scared
and it took her two years to make up her mind.

'The Bodyguard'
is the story of a pop star called Rachel
and her bodyguard Frank.
The film has action and romance.
It was a big success.
By the end of 1992
it had made £135 million in the UK.
It went on to make
$400 million world-wide.

The album from the film
was just as successful.
It broke the record
for the most albums sold in one week.

One beautiful song is at the centre of
the album. That song is
'I Will Always Love You'.
It was the best selling single of 1992
and the third best in 1993!

Whitney in the film 'The Bodyguard'.

'I Will Always Love You'
is the No 1 song played at funerals.

In the UK,
a woman was taken to court
for playing the single over and over again
day and night.

After the birth of Bobbi Kristina,
Whitney set off on another world tour.
Bobby and their daughter
joined her on stage.
Old fans and new ones
came to hear her sing one song:
'I Will Always Love You'.
It is a show stopper.

She won eight more music awards
and another Grammy
for songs from 'The Bodyguard'.
It was the second biggest selling album ever.

Whitney spent 1994
touring the USA and south Africa.
She and Bobby
made their first single together
called 'Something In Common'.
In it Bobby sings:
'Girl you know it's you I adore'
and she sings:
'And there's no-one in this world
that I love more'.

Bobby and Whitney's marriage
has not always been
as perfect as the song says.
They separated in 1995.
He was seen in a club with another woman
and without his wedding ring.
Soon after, he went into a clinic
to try and get free from drugs and drink.
When he came out Whitney took him back.

She said:
'I've got a good man.
He takes care of me.'
To prove it she has an 11-carat diamond ring
on her finger.
It was given to her by Bobby.

7 Still at the Top

Her next film came out in 1995 –
it was 'Waiting to Exhale'.
It tells the story of one difficult year
in the lives of four successful black women.
They are looking for good men.

The album from the film
has three new Whitney tracks on it.

In May 1996
she finished filming 'The Preacher's Wife'.
The album came out in November.
It's a mix of gospel and pop.

Whitney has always wanted
to go back to her musical roots
and make an album of gospel music.
She didn't know it would be the music
from one of her films.
Again Cissy sings on the album
and so does Bobby
with his re-formed New Edition.

In the film,
Whitney plays Julia,
a young mother and the preacher's wife.
They have problems
and the preacher prays for help.

An angel, played by Denzil Washington
comes into their lives.
The romantic and funny story
starts from there.

Sadly, Whitney had a miscarriage
in January 1997.
But she didn't stop working.
She says:
'You have all these people around,
but in the long run,
it's down to you.'

She came to the UK in March
to sing on the National Lottery show.
She sang her new single
'I Believe In You And Me'.
It's from 'The Preacher's Wife' album.
Then she set off on a tour of the Far East.

Whitney's next film is said
to be the story of an under-cover cop
who cracks a drugs ring.

In 1997 she was given
her twenty-first American Music Award.
This is a record.
No-one has more awards than her.

She is still at the top
but in the 1990s her output of records
has been slow.

Whitney has spent a lot of time
sorting out her stormy marriage.
In March 1997
she saw Bobby
flirting with Spice Girl, Mel B.
She told Bobby's manager
to throw the Spice Girls CD away.

Whitney said:
'I didn't get married to play a game.
You don't play a game
with bringing life into this world.'

If she can tame the wild man of rap
she will have more time
to give to her work and her fans.

I Came to Coventry
An Autobiography

W. H. Barnes

JANUS PUBLISHING COMPANY
London, England

First published in Great Britain 1994
by Janus Publishing Company
Duke House, 37 Duke Street
London W1M 5DF

British Library Cataloguing in Publication Data
A catalogue record for this book is available
from the British Library.

ISBN 1 85756 101 5

Cover design Harold King

Phototypeset by Intype, London
Printed and bound in England by Antony Rowe Ltd,
Chippenham, Wiltshire

THE "BARNES" LINE
FROM C. 1700 A.D.

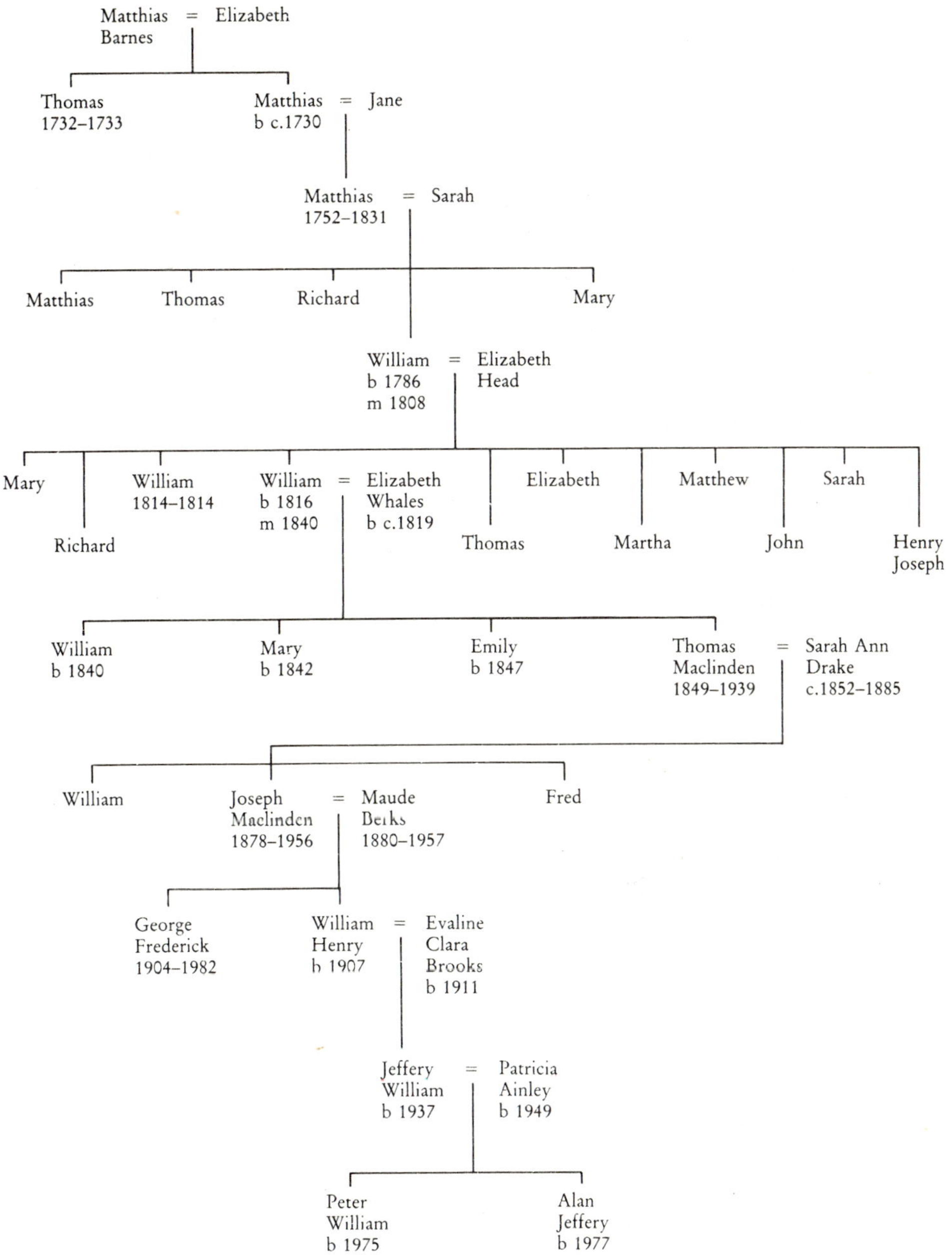

ANTECEDENTS OF PE
(FROM GREAT-GREAT GRAN

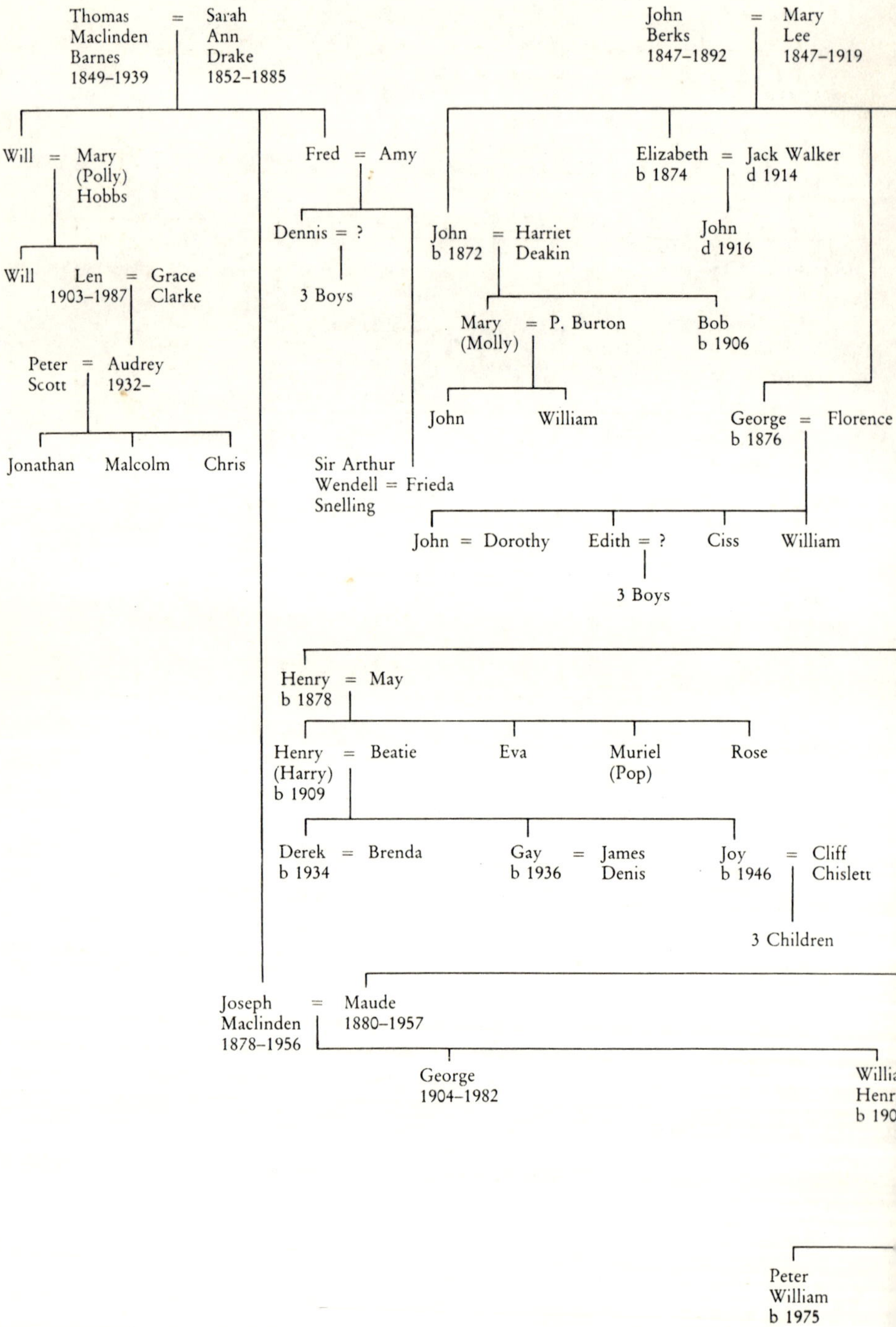

ALAN BARNES
RENTS IN MALE LINE)

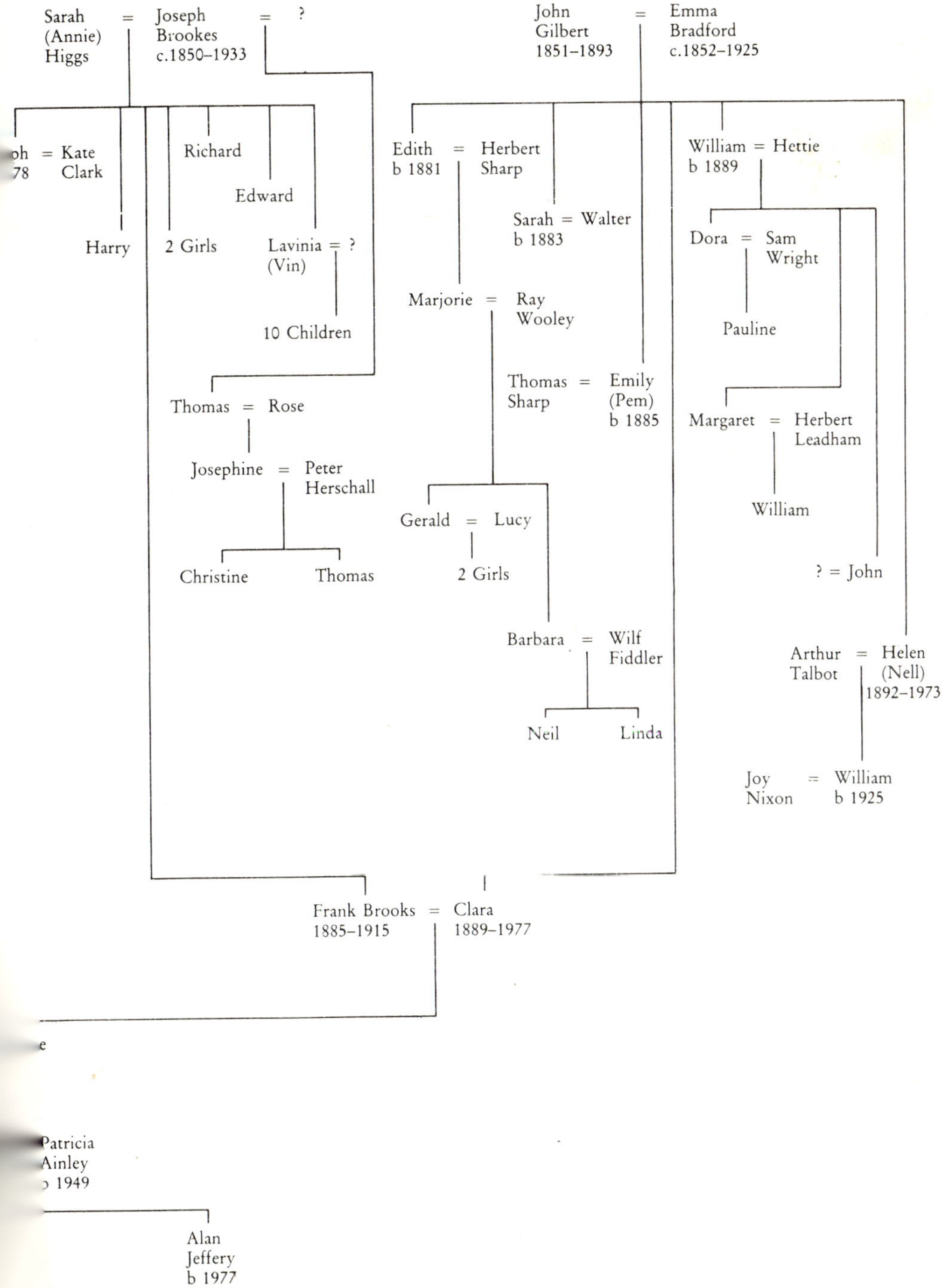

Chapter One

I was in my late sixties when I decided, after some persuasion, to give you, my son and grandchildren, an account of some of the personalities, interesting and otherwise, who have played a part in my life, some of whom are ancestors from whom you are certain to have inherited a few characteristics of intellect and personal appearance.

I shall try to describe events which come to my mind – separate pictures and sketches which, when revolved in the kaleidoscope of time, combine to build up an image of the changes through which I have lived. These impressions range through a revolutionary period of history, beginning with the Edwardian period into which I was born, followed by the stresses, sorrows, disappointments and triumphs of the two World Wars and ending in the modern times into which the younger members of my family have been born.

My paternal forebears have been traced by my son, Jeffery, something I promised myself that I would do, but the excuse was easier than the effort. Jeff undertook this work after he came down from university and quite a number of visits were paid to Somerset House, the Public Record office etc. In this respect Jeff had a lot of help and assistance from his cousin Audrey, my cousin Len's daughter who worked in the West End and often, I understand, went without her lunch to follow up some lead. Many letters were written to parish parsons from whom great help was received and churches visited to inspect baptismal records. The necessary evidence was found tracing the male line back to about 1720, some nine generations. Very largely these forebears seem to have been 'Men of Kent', as indeed my father was.

I have no personal knowledge of earlier ancestors, other than those shown by the family tree, before my grandfather,

Thomas McLinden Barnes. He married Sarah Ann Drake in London in 1876. He was a stonemason and my father asserts that he was a good tradesman. He worked, according to Father, on many cathedral churches, but soon after his marriage he joined the army. He joined as a 'single' man – I believe married men were not accepted at that time. He joined in the false name of Jackson, knowing he could then desert if he found the service life not to his liking. He left his wife and son with her parents.

In fact, he liked the life and later declared his true name and also declared his marriage to obtain the payment due to a wife. He therefore had two different dates of marriage, but with the army date apparently making the first-born illegitimate. This confused the family researches, but we finally obtained a true marriage certificate to redeem the family honour.

Grandfather Mac had joined the Royal Engineers and at a later date was posted to the West Indies. By this time there were four children; William, Joseph McLinden, Charles Frederick and Ciss; the youngest dying in infancy. My father, the second-born, often talked to me of his stay in Bermuda and how he spent so much time swimming in those clear warm waters. He also said that they called at New York going out, but did not go ashore. They could not have been in Bermuda more than two years when they suffered the sad loss of their mother. She was buried in the military cemetery. I have seen a photograph of the grave, showing a nice stone which grandfather had erected – the inscription on the stone being very clear. The children were soon despatched back to England. I gather my father, being the elder, felt very responsible on the voyage home, the eldest, William, having been left at home in England. There is no record of Ciss' death, but I believe the boys settled down quite happily with their mother's parents at Chatham. Grandfather Drake worked in the dockyard there.

My father had a defective right eye which, I understand, was caused by a difficult birth, and later thwarted his strong wish to join the army. He never lost his early love of the service and I can recall when we lived at Whittington, of which more anon, which has a barracks a mile or so from the village, he would listen to the bugle calls and tell me what they meant. Alas, thirty years later I had had too much bugle and army discipline and no affection.

In due course Grandfather returned from the West Indies and presumably, to the surprise of the children, brought home with him a new wife, apparently a former soldier's widow. They settled at Colchester, a garrison town, to which I have paid a few visits. My wife was very thrilled with the castle and its Roman remains on a visit a few years ago. The grandparents, I expect, were not sorry to shed the responsibility of the children, but the latter, I learned, did not share this view. Few step-mothers evoke in their young charges the love of the real mother and in this case a positive dislike took place. My father told me that his step-mother was Welsh and 'like the rest of that nationality, never to be trusted'. This obsession remained with him all his life and more than once he said to me, 'my lad, never trust a Welshman'. It sounded to me like an echo of Dickens, 'Sammy me boy, never trust a Vider'.

Father talked little of his school-days but later I was to have great respect for his general knowledge. Uncle Will went into engineering and Uncle Fred received a better education but thwarted his father's ambitions by running off and joining the army: the Royal Engineers, of course. He married an officer's daughter and himself retired as a Lieutenant Colonel. They had two children, Dennis and Frieda. Both did very well for themselves, as I will relate in due course. Uncle Will had two sons, the elder was killed in the 1914 war while still under age for service. The younger one, Len, I am still in touch with.

My father must have been apprenticed to the building trade and left home at an early age, as was to be expected, and apparently moved around quite a lot. While still quite young he came to Staffordshire. His employers had a contract at Whittington Barracks, the depot of the North & South Staffs regiment. He obtained digs in the village and there met my mother. Whether his courting did not go too well or whether due to the necessity of following the work, I don't know, but his next stop was Huddersfield. He enjoyed himself in Yorkshire, I believe. He joined madrigal and glee societies; this being pleasure at minimal cost. I suppose the alternative in those days was loneliness or pubs.

It was not very long before he was back in the Lichfield district, maybe the pangs of love brought him back or again the necessity of work. They were married on 1st June, 1903 and, as a good story-book says, lived happily ever after.

The trials and tribulations of their class in the first quarter of the twentieth century must have been quite horrifying. It is difficult to understand why they did not all become strong radicals. Father has said to me that the working man's great enemy is ignorance; as the poet Thomas Gray said:

But knowledge to their eyes her ample page
  Rich with the spoils of time did ne'er unroll;
Chill penury repress'd their noble rage,
  And froze genial current of the soul

Chapter Two

George Frederick, my parents' first-born, arrived on third April, 1904, and I, William Henry, was born on sixth December, 1907. My mother's parents came from Burntwood to Whittington, our birthplace. Grandfather Berks was the baker at Burntwood asylum. After their marriage in 1870 they bought a business at Whittington – this being a bakery and village store. They must have prospered initially – there were three horses and carts delivering bread to villages as far apart as Elford and Edingale. My mother's father originally came from Burslem in the Potteries, his wife from a small village called Willey, near Rugby. They had five children, what I suppose must be called a small brood in those days of large families – indeed we had one family in the village of no fewer than twenty-three children. Many writers assert that it is difficult to separate fact from fiction when recalling one's earliest memories. I have been told that I have a fair memory and certainly my school-days seem very clear to me.

My grandparents' five children were John, Elizabeth, George, Henry and Maude, the last being my mother. The house and shop they bought was very old and I told my father it must have been old when Adam was a lad. This property has recently been cleared away and the village altered out of all recognition. The business was closed by the time I was around but the house was still lived in.

Grandfather Berks had bought five cottages, one for each child, but his efforts achieved no lasting benefit. There were several hard winters, I understand, and the consequent unemployment had its effect – as did, I suspect, grandfather's warm heart: he could not see his customers want, and their ability to pay later was negligible. In addition to this, one of his horses strayed on to the railway line and was killed and another broke its neck in the stable. Grandfather died at a comparatively early age in 1892 when the business must have closed down.

Uncle Harry made an effort to revive the bakery side, because I can remember his working in the bakehouse kneading the dough and handling the long peel to place and retrieve the loaves from the oven. I was intrigued to see him dig his elbow into the cottage-type loaves. This was standard practice and not considered unhygienic. He always looked very old when working because inevitably his moustache and eyebrows were covered in flour. When his efforts came to an end and baking was finished for good, we children had the scope for playing hide and seek in the dough bins and in the big oven. I was caught in the oven once by another uncle and given a strong lecture on the dangers of the oven roof collapsing. This, I understand, was not unusual – or rather, it wasn't with those old ovens. The interior, as I remember it, was about twelve feet square with a low, arched roof of bricks – we had to kneel when inside.

We had numerous cousins in the village. Uncle Jack had a son, Bob, and a daughter, Mary; Uncle George, two sons and two daughters; Jack, Bill, Edith and Ciss. Uncle Harry, one son and three daughters; Harry, Eva, Muriel and Rose, and Aunt Ciss one son. This cousin died when he was sixteen. Bob, Harry and I were always together, being of a similar age. Harry was the star turn; his escapades were legendary and his humour infectious. As a youngster his progression to swear-words was quite rapid, considerably hastened by an uncle or cousin (where or how he fitted into the family I don't know) who came on a visit just once. He gave Harry a penny for each swear-word and his vocabulary raced along and he earned a sixpenny piece. We had no compunction in helping him spend his ill-gotten gains. This relative's name was Jack Weldon and many years later our family received a newspaper announcing his death. He was then Chief of Police in Hong Kong and I recall that one whole page was devoted to his passing.

Our life at Whittington was quite happy despite father's periodic unemployment. We lived quite well, we often ate hares, rabbits and wood pigeons, which cost us nothing.

It would be appropriate now to recall a few very far-off memories. We were once paddling in a farmer's pond and after a while we went to get our boots. Another boy shouted for one of us to throw him his boots: Harry did so, but misaimed and one boot went into the pond, never to be seen again. This was a serious loss, the boy who had lost a boot was one of the twenty-three and Harry had to circumnavigate his way to school for some time to avoid the other boy's parents.

On another occasion a number of us were lying in a field, no doubt enjoying the warm sun after much exertion, when Harry, true to form, tied Ernie Ballanger's leg to a tree without his knowing. Then Harry jumped up and shouted 'look up, here's the bull'. We were on our feet in an instant and so was Ernie but he was soon on the turf again, shouting 'he's got me'. Harry then shouted 'it's alright, it's only Big Molly, the red cow', which, of course, he had known all the time.

Harry became a pillar of the village church and only recently I was looking at a very pretty inscribed clock, presented to him in recognition of his twenty years' service as church-warden and chairman of the parochial church council. He was also clerk to the parish for many years, and is secretary of a local charity and most impartial in his assessment of need, subject to the Charity Commissioners' approval; his reformation is thus complete.

I can recall the outbreak of the 1914 war and the great excitement, but later great unhappiness. Troops were billeted in the village and the farm next to our house had its quota, including horses. They were ASC later to become the RASC (Royal Army Service Corps). We boys were surprised to see how well the horses were groomed, hooves polished as well as the harness. The soldiers wore puttees, and chin-straps to keep their headgear on.

Movement of troops was frequent and our visits up to the barracks were many, and I remember how proud I felt walking alongside a column marching in splendid order. Often a battalion would be marching to Trent Valley station, Lichfield, en route for goodness-knows-where, headed by the regimental band playing rousing yet poignant tunes. Sometimes pith helmets were carried, strapped to each soldier's back, indicating obviously a warmer clime. It is an unwritten law in the army that no one breaks a column on the march, but on one occasion I was on my bike and wanted to cross the road, so cycled in between two companies: the shouting and language that assailed me!

When conscription was introduced, Father was called for his medical examination. He came and informed Mother than he had been declined because of heart trouble. This news caused great concern to Mother and she quickly suggested a visit to the family doctor. This gentleman said that he could find nothing wrong with Father and he would have passed him if he had been on the medical board. About twelve months later when the manpower shortage was becoming more acute, all men previously declined had to have another medical examination. Father duly went and was passed A1 despite the fact that he could not see out of his right eye.

To have some choice of unit or arm of the service it was permissible to join before being called, so Father made his choice, joining the RFC, (Royal Flying Corps), later to become the RAF. Events seemed to happen very quickly and we were quite dumbfounded when Mother told us that Father would be leaving us in two days' time. I was informed much later in happier times that my remark on hearing this news was 'I shall have to have a good look at him tonight'. He was back home in four weeks on embarkation leave and subsequently he arrived in Egypt. This was a very unhappy period for us, as for so many. George and I could see how thin and forlorn Mother was through worry. She obtained a job in the military hospital at the barracks and we often went to meet her there. I speculated later how stretched the authorities must have been at this time, living as we did almost in the centre of England, and yet soldiers arrived at this hospital caked in Flanders mud.

One incident in the Great War remains in my memory. Mother got up during the night when George and I were asleep and, hearing a strange noise, she looked out of the window and saw an unusual sight for that day and age: an aeroplane flying over. We learned the next day that it had been a German bomber aircraft and it had dropped bombs on Walsall a few miles from where we lived in Lichfield. I believe very few planes were used for bombing by either side. The Jerries of course had the Zeppelins and they were used in bombing raids many times, mainly on London. When my wife was about six years old, she went to London for a holiday and saw Zeppelins several times.

However, time passed, and the day arrived when we heard that the war was over. Our vicar promptly called a service of thanksgiving, and Mother went to church, George saying that we would do the housework. While cleaning the kitchen I remarked to George 'this will be a tale to tell our children'. We did that housework on the first Armistice Day, 11 November, 1918.

Father was demobilised the following February. Mother met us coming from school, or rather she met me, George having left school by this time, and I learned that Dad was at Southampton and would be home in a day or two. Unfortunately Granny died and she was buried the day after Dad arrived home. Among several presents he brought us was an Egyptian watch each for my brother and me. I never tired of asking questions about what Father had seen and done. He told me that he had travelled from the French Channel coast to the toe of Italy in a cattle truck by rail and then by ship to Alexandria.

I have later in life felt pleased that I was born in the country and was not, therefore, a town sparrow. Country children, it seems to me, grow up with a greater love and appreciation of natural phenomena. We boys went far and wide through fields and woods looking for birds' nests and squirrels' dreys; we were so adept at tree climbing, we thought nothing of it. One or more of our many relatives would take us for long walks on Sundays and we learned the country names of flowers and grasses. The botanical names, of which I only know a few, seem to lose the romance and fun of the country names, such as Creeping Jenny, Ladies' Needlework, Meadow Sweet, Granny's Bonnet, Old Man's Beard and scores more. My interest in birds has never diminished and my wife and I get a lot of pleasure these days walking in the country with our binoculars. Looking out of the window at this moment I see a song thrush, a great tit, a wren and others.

A friend of mine of long ago whom I must mention was Charlie Mann. His parents kept the farm near to us. I was always welcome at the farm, had some meals with them and sometimes slept there. There were two daughters, Dolly and Mary, who were older, quite attractive, and good pianists. Charlie could do most jobs on the farm, from milking to ploughing, and these experiences gave me great pleasure. I recall sitting in a pear tree one day with Charlie and eating more fruit than was good for us, with the inevitable result.

Before Father came back from the war George had obtained a job for himself. He was a big, strong lad and quite fearless. The man who kept the local hotel had a smart horse and trap and George had to take two girls from the village to the girls' High School at Lichfield every day. The horse was very spritely but the duties were performed without mishap. Another of his tasks was to attend to a single Hereford cow which the hotelier had obtained and grazed in an adjacent field. George had to milk the cow, with little or no experience of such work. Having caught the animal, one of us had to hold her and the other got under her. To hold a cow in the open the recognised way was to stand in front of the animal and grip a horn with the left hand with the right hand holding the nostrils. After a while I asked George how he was doing and he replied 'she won't give any, you have a go', and so we changed over and then we changed again. After what must have been a good half an hour we managed to cover the bottom of the pail. George took this back and told his boss he thought the cow was dry.

Chapter Three

It is a common cliché for people to remark on changes since their youth, but looking back over five or six decades I find the small things so noticeable. Birds will remain pecking in the grass on the roadside now, with traffic thundering past, and young people ride horses through traffic with complete nonchalance – in my young days the reverse applied. Horses were very frightened and to meet a threshing engine or a steamroller with a horse-drawn cart was something to be avoided. I have seen a man stop and take off his jacket and put it over the horse's head and hang on to the bridle until the danger had passed. Horses frequently took fright, and it required no little courage to try and stop a runaway. Uncle George, my mother's brother, would attempt it by chasing the animal on his bicycle.

Soon after Father's return from the war he discussed the question of us moving from the village. His primary object I know was the welfare of George and me, but to me the idea was repugnant from every point of view. When I tried to remonstrate father replied, in no uncertain terms, 'You will never earn a decent living in the middle of a forest, lad'. This remark lingered with me and I have often wondered whether he thought of the village as a forest, excluding worldly contact. We did move to Lichfield and I was soon in a new school and hating every bit of it.

Two things relieved the gloom: firstly I got on well with one master, Mr Armstrong, this I think was because I was good at arithmetic. It amuses me these days to hear fond parents refer to their offspring's progress in mathematics – is it audacity or ignorance – maths starts later. The second thing was that my football ability met with approval. I went to this new school for about three years and soon after starting there Mr Armstrong strongly advised me to sit the entrance examination for the grammar school: he said he was sure I would pass easily. I trust the reader will forgive me when I say I think his assessment was right but, fool that I was, I said no and lived to regret it. In all modesty, I know my classmates who went on to the grammar school to have been not quite as intelligent.

The reason I declined this wonderful opportunity was class-consciousness, the curse of so many of my generation. We lived in a very small house opposite the grammar school, and Lichfield was a very snooty place at that time. The school was largely filled with the sons of well-to-do people. By a strange irony, some years later when I was doing quite well in Coventry, I met one of these former students; we thought we recognised each other and on learning who I was it was his turn to be embarrassed – he was emptying gas meters. I left school in due course with little hope and no prospects and Father said I must go to night school. This I did and quite enjoyed it. My former head schoolmaster informed me that a boy was wanted at a shop in the town – they accepted me and much to father's disgust I started in shop life at five shillings weekly and my parents told me that I was in a dead-end job – my prospects were as limited as my education. However, I stayed at this shop for about four and a half years; it was a high-class outfitters and furnishers and we regularly served a number of titled customers. At eighteen years of age I was only earning twelve and six weekly.

I continually wrote after possible jobs and very nearly secured one in the local LMS railway, but it was a false trail. Eventually a commercial traveller informed me of a vacancy at Tamworth in the same line of business; I obtained this job and was elated to be earning two pounds per week. I bought a new cycle and cycled the nine miles to Tamworth.

About this time I got interested in dancing. I soon learned to dance and, I recall, took the young lady pianist in the dance band home one night. I carried her music satchel and got her home safely and then hurried home – it seemed I was coming on a bit – but she never agreed to me taking her home again. At the time I could not understand this, but I grew wiser.

The man I worked for at Tamworth, Mr White, was a great character and I was happy. My two main interests at this time were tennis and dancing and both were enjoyed as far as my limited income would allow.

Mother now talked to me seriously about money, my capital being nil. She suggested that I save ten shillings weekly and I said I would give one pound for my keep. In addition, I put by five shillings for clothing – fortunately cigarettes were cheap. The wisdom of mother's advice was seen later and I have always been grateful for it.

Tamworth is quite different to Lichfield, or at least it was in 1927. The class distinction in Lichfield was repugnant but the reverse in Tamworth did not please me, probably I was a bit of a snob in some ways. I have always appreciated well-spoken English and ungrammatical speech to me is tiresome. General speech in Tamworth was quite poor and the miners had a vocabulary all of their own. It was here one day I met an early village schoolfriend who had attended Lichfield Grammar School and who was now articled to a solicitor. He spoke to me with such affable assurance that my self-criticism was refuelled.

I had had pianoforte lessons from about age eleven and later joined the local town band, playing the cornet. We did not obtain many engagements, but playing at village flower shows were happy events.

I stated, when I started this mammoth task, that I would endeavour to write a family history, but I am becoming increasingly aware that it is merely autobiographical.

To my son Jeffery, and grandsons Peter and Alan, the ultimate recipients of this book, I say I know no other way how to achieve the desired end. I will inform you of all the relations I have met through the years when our paths crossed.

Mr White, for whom I worked at Tamworth, had bought another business at Coventry, hence his need for me. After some two years he decided to sell the property and the business closed. When this happened I obtained a similar job in Banbury. The owner of this business was completely different to Mr White. He owned two shops and I looked after the smaller one. My weekly wage was two pounds and five shillings and now I had to find and pay for lodgings. I found a place on the Warwick Road that would take me in for one pound weekly: it was quite a humble and modest home.

This was my first night away from home: much has been written about young people stepping out into the world, and to me it was quite momentous. Fear of the unexpected was not in any way part of my outlook, but I was dreadfully homesick. During that first night in a strange house I could not sleep. Continual moaning was coming from some adjacent room. The breakfast provided was reasonable and then I asked what the moaning was, and the reply was that 'grandmother was dying'. My bag was soon packed, and having asked the amount owed, I informed them I should not be back.

It was clear I could not afford the accommodation I desired on my present income, so I decided to beard the lion in his den. Having acquainted my new employer with my predicament I made a request for a modest increase in salary. I had to listen to a torrent of abuse and obtained no rise. New digs did, however, appear out of the blue and very splendid they were, for twenty-five shillings weekly.

My employer continued to provoke me and one day he came into my shop and got very personal. I told him what I thought of him and so he gave me notice to leave in a week. My stay in Banbury had been just four weeks, but for years it depressed me to go near the place.

Arriving back in Lichfield I was very subdued; the one bright spot being I would see my girlfriend, Evaline. We had met at dances before the traumatic Banbury experience. She wore her hair in ringlets down her back, but she arrived at one dance with her hair in a fashionable bob, and I immediately thought how splendid she looked, and lost no time in booking the last waltz with her, and taking her home. The Cathedral clock was striking twelve o'clock before I left her and I said 'I am twenty-one today' and so I bade her goodnight. We arranged to meet the following Sunday evening on a certain railway bridge, but unfortunately I caught the flu and was soon confined to bed. How to let my Evaline know was a poser. However, brother George and his young lady, in whom I had to confide, put the matter right.

After a few days at home on returning from Banbury, I was to be found in Tamworth again, and, having explained my position to my old employer, he suggested I should rejoin him for the duration of the closing-down sale. This suggestion was very acceptable although only temporary. Mr White came one morning with the Coventry paper and showed me an advertisement for an appointment which he thought would suit me. The application was made and an interview arranged for the following Sunday – and behold, the job was mine.

It was a very nice shop doing a high-class trade including silk top hats. My salary was fifty shillings. The search for suitable lodgings began once more. My stay at the first place I took was of even shorter duration than my former experience. Having left my case at the house and returning to the shop I was informed that my lunch break would be twelve till one p.m., so at noon I set forth to appease my appetite. On arrival at my selected abode the dining-room seemed awful and I found myself sitting next to a very undesirable character, so I paid for the meal and collected my bag, but in the same street I found more suitable accommodation.

Chapter Four

Before I tell you more of my life in Coventry, chronological order will have to be broken. I must tell you how we came to meet two different families. When we were still at Whittington, Mother and Father decided to visit Willey, this being the village Granny Berks came from. Present-day children will scarcely believe me when I say at this time I had not been more than three miles from my birthplace, so it can be imagined how a journey of thirty-five miles appealed. I think I would be about ten years old and George would be fourteen. Mother and I went by train and George and Dad cycled. To be on a train was a great thrill, to see the guard wave his green flag and blow his whistle was quite new – and I poked my head out of the window, of course. Rugby station, where we had to change trains, appeared gigantic. We soon arrived at the village of Ullesthorpe and walked across the fields to Willey. Mother's cousin met us, and to my surprise there were Dad and George. These relations we boys called Uncle Tom and Aunty Polly, their family being quite grown up.

Uncle Tom was the carpenter on an estate some way outside the village. He took me on his cycle to the Hall and various other places. He was a humorous chap and had a never-ending fund of stories to tell. One of these concerned a local burial; Uncle told me he had been a bearer. All had gone well until they were lowering the coffin into the grave when Uncle let go of his rope and the coffin finished up perpendicular instead of horizontal.

This, my first holiday, I remember so well. These relations died and we did not keep in touch with the next generation. Just for the record, their name was Wright. A year or two ago we were motoring through these villages when we saw a well-established garage in the name of 'Wright'. We did not stop but I speculated on a possible connection.

The second family meeting was quite different. It would be about 1922. Father decided we should visit his parents and great excitement ensued. We caught a London train at Trent Valley station and I was full of questions. This habit of asking so many questions had been a life-long habit, and, I realise, not always a popular one, but Dad encouraged it. We arrived at Euston, our first visit to London, in great wonder. With suitable advice from Father as to where we put our feet, we proceeded down the steps and into a lift, then quickly sank into the bowels of the earth. We emerged from there and walked along to an escalator. At this time they were peculiar to London and a modern wonder to me. Then by tube train to the station at Liverpool Street and we proceeded to Colchester.

Grandfather Barnes met us at the station and I didn't know what to think of him. He would have been seventy-two at this time, about five feet seven inches tall, very broad, stocky and upright. He greeted George and me with minimum words and effect, put his arms round my mother and father and walked out of the station and we trailed behind. Then we all got on a bus for West Bergholt and arrived in half an hour at the bungalow 'Penslade', Chapel Lane – and then met Grandmother. The bungalow was not very large and was built of wood on a brick foundation.

The following day Father's younger brother came, so we had Uncle Fred, Aunt Amy and cousins, Dennis and Frieda. Uncle was then a captain in the REs. They had spent a number of years in Africa and I believe the children had been born there. Uncle was a well-built man and looked typically like an army man. Aunt Amy was fairly tall and I suppose sophisticated. Unfortunately, on the third day, Frieda caught measles and was confined to her room. I played with Dennis, who was a few years younger than myself. Aunt and Uncle were put up at a nearby bungalow. We have never met Dennis or Frieda again, but I have met their parents several times.

Dennis eventually went into the army via Woolwich – and

non-army people will wonder what that means. It is simply that army commissions for the infantry are obtained through Sandhurst but for higher units through Woolwich. Dennis was commissioned into the Royal Artillery. We saw a photograph of him in the daily press in 1940 when at Dunkirk he had obtained the Military Cross. The photograph showed him with his bride. They subsequently had three sons.

Frieda eventually went to London University and obtained a degree in Economics, and while there she met another cousin and they married. He also obtained a good degree in Economics and then passed the higher Civil Service examination. This particular exam is only open to graduates, I understand. Frieda had several babies I believe, but I did not hear of any surviving.

While at West Bergholt, George took photographs with his box-plate camera and one photo was very good, a group of all of us – but, alas, it has since been lost. Also on this holiday we went to Clacton-on-Sea and Father swam round the pier. I remember being very impressed with the expanse of sea, and recall what a lot of roses were grown in Essex and how light the soil was. We actually had two holidays at West Bergholt and they were the only times I saw these grandparents. I will now make an effort to resume chronological order.

Chapter Five

My life in Coventry was quite happy and I made some good friends. The young chap next in age to me at 'Batts' (that was the shop-owner's name, and the nearest approach to an educated ferret I have ever seen) was Frank Redgrave, a grand lad and a gentleman, and we are today, about fifty years later, still very good friends.

The Coventry of 1930 and today bear little resemblance. When I first knew it, it seemed to be lingering in the nineteenth century but in some respects it was very modern. In 1930 I enjoyed very much a performance in the Old Cathedral of Handel's *Messiah*. Coventry has some very notable ancient buildings: I suppose the best is St Mary's Hall, where I believe Mary Queen of Scots was lodged on her way to Fotheringhay. Another recollection of my early acquaintance with this city is its smells, now almost non-existent. I have read that the human sense of smell is the most memory-provoking and I believe this to be so and can recall the smell of heated metal and from Courtauld's the smell produced by the spinning of viscose fibre at their Foleshill factory.

I went home each Saturday night, we closed the shop at nine p.m. and by train arrived home at midnight. Sunday was spent almost exclusively with Eva. We walked miles in the country and I know we were very much in love. To be beautiful and intelligent I believe to be rare qualities. She also read a lot and liked good verse. Back in Coventry I walked to discover the City and to save money and dream of the day I could ask Eva to marry me.

In 1930 the trade depression was severe and it progressively worsened until the figure reached three million unemployed. Alas, after eighteen months at Batts, trade was so bad I joined this vast horde together with two more of the staff. This was one of the really unhappy periods of my life; to want so much, marriage, a home, etc., and to obtain so little. But my one great good fortune, Eva, did not desert me, much to my father's surprise, though his respect and liking for her was considerable.

I was unemployed for about one year despite all my endeavours. During this period someone suggested that I could try London for a job. Eva's Aunt Kit and Uncle Joe put me up for several days: they lived in Hornsey Rise in North London. My many applications for work came to nothing. At one interview I was asked what wages I expected and replied two pounds fifty; they laughed and said 'pass on; we can't pay that sort of money'. The queue of applicants was endless. This was a very depressing business and one day I thought to relieve the monotony by a visit to the House of Commons. I had no ticket, so I just queued up and soon found myself in the public gallery, and was extremely thrilled. The debate concerned Imperial Preference and was following Mr Baldwin's return from the Ottawa Conference. I saw and heard many of the leading parliamentary figures of the day, including Ramsay MacDonald, Mr Foot (father of Michael Foot) and a number of others. I left the Commons at about eleven-thirty p.m. and when Uncle Joe and Aunt Kit saw me they were quite relieved. They quite thought I had got lost in the big city.

It is well ordained by a benevolent providence that human beings have no prevision of the future, otherwise my zest for living might have evaporated. My brother got married in 1930, his wife being a farmer's daughter. The farm, being about three miles outside Lichfield at a village called Chorley, was within easy cycling distance for me, and having nothing else to do I often went there. I got on well with my sister-in-law's parents and was quite happy to lend a hand on the farm.

Each evening I was waiting at the City station to meet Eva off the Birmingham train, and to see her looking so smart and capable and myself unemployed was a terrible trial. It is quite easy to recall my thoughts of this period and I remember thinking: it can't go on like this, will it improve or worsen?

The country was in a terrible state and hunger marches from the depressed areas to London were taking place.

Mother and Father were extremely kind and never levelled any criticism at me. Brother George made a number of suggestions such as working with him in the building trade, but I shuddered at the thought. He did, however, come up with the idea that put me on the road to success. The man living next door to George was a superintendent with the Prudential and George arranged for me to meet him and to hear what possibilities there might be for me. I was most impressed with what this man told me, but the great difficulty was where to find a vacancy. Lichfield had none and the age limit was twenty-five. I had not previously thought of insurance in any way. My visits to nearby towns failed to find a Prudential vacancy. One day I got a letter from my former colleagues of Coventry, asking me to come to a birthday party. My father suggested I should go, and, while there, apply to the local Prudential office.

My friend Frank Redgrave's mother put me up for the night and next morning I went into the Prudential office. At this time there were two Pru offices in Coventry. The one I went into was the district office, Coventry East, which dealt with claims etc. The head clerk told me there were no vacancies at present and so I was quickly despatched. I was walking along the pavement in Queens Road when two men overtook me and asked me if I was looking for a job with the Company and I informed them that was what I had been about. The older one of the two gave me his card and told me to go back and to see the District Manager and present his card. The same clerk met me in the office and having told him what I wanted and presented the card I obtained the desired interview.

The District Manager was very pleasant and said I was the type of young man they wanted but regretted that there was no immediate opening. After some thought he asked me if I had tried at the other local office and I told him I had not. He then picked up the phone and spoke to the other District Manager, a Mr Bridgstock. He told me where this office was and to make my way there for another interview. In a short while I was at 33 Hertford Street and found Mr Bridgstock to be a very smart and efficient man. I was taken into a small private office and given a more searching interview. I sensed there could be something in the wind here and that I should succeed or fail by my own bearing and responses. He plied me with questions – why did I think I might make a good insurance man – did I know the district of Radford – was I good at figures, what was seven and a half per cent of three hundred and seventy-five pounds. I was really on my toes and felt that I was making an impression. He then informed me that there would be an agency vacant in two weeks' time and did I want it. I replied 'most certainly'.

We then completed official forms and I was taken to a Dr Soden for a medical examination. Mr Bridgstock gave me a letter to take to the Prudential Divisional Office in Birmingham where I saw the Divisional Manager and then completed a written educational test. To my great delight I was told the job was mine.

I had previously arranged with Eva that I would look for her at the Dolcis shoe shop in Corporation Street and indicate success or otherwise by the thumbs up or down; my success provoked a beaming smile. Young people today might wonder why she could not meet me and talk, but alas, in 1932 this was forbidden, shop life was very strict – even use of Christian names was forbidden.

Mother and Father were also delighted and after ten days or so I received a telegram from Coventry telling me to report on a certain day to take up my duties. My cycle would be an asset there so I cycled to Coventry. The Company, as I shall now refer to my employers, worked what was known as the 'block' system. It means that each agent has a defined area which he controls, drawn on the office map, and which makes for economical running. New business could be written anywhere but it had to be transferred to the agent whose area it was, after so many weeks.

Mr Collier, the Assistant Superintendent, showed me round and taught me all he knew for several weeks. I stayed with the

Redgrave family for four weeks and then found myself digs on my agency. Mr Collier said that I should provide myself with a desk and he sold me one that he had for four pounds or so, a very nice rolled-top type. For several weeks I did not know whether I was on my head or my heels. Each Wednesday it was necessary to see Mr Bridgstock: he could see that I was keen to learn and he lent me a number of books on insurance and so, gradually, I progressed.

The Company also ran an Approved Society for National Health Insurance. There were about five hundred calls on my agency and some six hundred members of our Approved Society, most of whom I called on for insurance premiums. My starting salary was three pounds weekly plus commission on new business, and twelve shillings and threepence a year for every thirteen NHI members. It was obligatory to deposit £50 with the Company as security. I recall that at that time I had £104, due to Mother's earlier advice on regular savings.

During my first week Mr Bridgstock and Mr Collier, who was soon to be moved and later promoted, had been out on my behalf and written some new business. Commission in those days was paid immediately from the agent's total collection of premiums. I went home for the weekend and Father was most curious to know how I had got on, and when I told him my total wages for the week he nearly fell off his chair. He lectured me strongly on honesty and said that no one in our family had ever 'gone wrong'. I had to convince him that the five pounds I had earned was quite legitimate.

Quickly seeing the possibilities in this business, I worked with a will, and at the end of June 1933 was top of the district for new business. This was not entirely due to my efforts. The Company provided a special salesman for each branch of our work – Industrial, Ordinary and General – and we were expected to submit prospects for their attention. They certainly did their quota for me.

The work I found most interesting, calling as we did on all types and classes of people and, as confidence grew between agent and client, I, like other agents, received many requests for advice and help on a variety of subjects, some of which were very amusing. Dealing with a death claim some years later I asked the widow if she had a solicitor and she replied, 'No, only you'.

Eva and I soon became engaged and she still loves the ring which I bought, a diamond solitaire. About a year or so after my commencing with the Company, Mr Bridgstock informed me that he would come out canvassing with me one evening. This event is recalled because of the following. He asked me if I had any ideas of marriage and, of course, I said 'very much so'. He then asked if I anticipated renting or buying a house. My reply was that I favoured buying, but so many new agents were here today and gone tomorrow, it made me hesitate. He put his hand on my shoulder and said 'You are here today and you will be here tomorrow' – so I started looking for a house.

The one we bought was newly built at Radford on the Moat House Estate. The original Moat House, which was being demolished, was the home of the Cash family, the makers of woven name tabs, etc. My house cost £525 and it was bought through the Hinckley and South Leicestershire Building Society, and my deposit was £50. During the final stages of building, I visited the house almost daily. Eva came to Coventry on her half-day holiday to pass her opinion on the house and she was quite delighted. My Superintendent at that time was Mr J. Coltman and he arranged with me to pick Eva up at Coventry station. We inspected the house and then Mr Coltman took us for tea to his home, 117 Browns Lane, and to meet his wife and baby daughter. John Coltman had a keen mind and a capacity for work seldom equalled; he remained my Superintendent until 1935, when he was again promoted. John and Gwen have remained our very good friends. The Company moved him many times and we visited them at Malvern, Leamington, Birmingham and Cardiff. They also had five different houses in Coventry and were experts at moving house.

Chapter Six

It seems to me now that my readers might like to know something of my wife's forebears. Her father was killed in the 1914–18 war very early. His parents came from Worcestershire, but of earlier people we have no knowledge. Grandfather Brooks and family lived in a village called Shrawley, but at one time he was a gamekeeper on Lord Salisbury's estate at Hatfield. This was the third Marquess and one of Britain's finest Foreign Secretaries and was three times Prime Minister. I have recently read a book, its title *The Later Salisburys*, and it is very well worth reading.

Unfortunately Grandmother Brooks died quite young, leaving seven children who were scattered to different relatives. I met in later years Uncle Joe, Uncle Harry and Aunt Vin but we'll discuss this later. Eva's father was sent to Newton Regis, near Tamworth, and brought up by a family whose precise relationship we have never discovered. Newton Regis was the home of my wife's mother's family. John Gilbert was a farm worker and he married Emma Bradford about 1875. They had six children – Edith, Sarah, Pem, Clara and Nellie, and a son William: I met all these aunts and uncles and, of course, their married partners. Again tragedy struck, Grandfather Gilbert being killed in 1894. He was drawing a heavy load with a team of horses at Fazeley when the horses took fright. He no doubt struggled frantically to control them because he had his small son with him: the boy was alright but his father died under the vehicle.

Granny Gilbert then had a very hard life having to bring up six children with such care and devotion. The relief which the parish gave was atrocious and a full day's washing brought in one shilling. I have always thought what an unusual bond of affection existed between the Gilbert sisters and brother and also the Brooks brothers and wonder if early tragedy accounts for this. Each family lost a parent very early and then my wife lost her father when only three years old.

My wife's father, after leaving school moved to Edinburgh. We have never discovered how or why this move came about, but as soon as he was old enough he joined the Seaforth Highland Regiment. It was probably the swishing kilt and bright uniform that impressed him. My wife's mother has often told me that Frank's love of Scotland and the Scots was very deep. He visited Newton Regis in his uniform when he was on leave and one can imagine the villagers being stirred by so unusual a sight. He spent several years in India and we have some very good photographs of his army life in the sub-continent.

When a soldier is demobilised after serving his chosen service, he has to remain on the army reserve for a few years, for which he receives a small payment. This reserve service was not quite finished when the 1914 war was declared and reservists were quickly recalled. Unfortunately, my father-in-law never returned. A few years ago I was speaking to someone who knew him. What he told me confirmed much of what I have read about the early period of the 1914–18 war. The Germans were so surprised at the efficiency of our firing they believed we had automatic weapons. Eva's father was wounded in November 1914 and died in Boulogne hospital in January 1915. Uncle Joe, his eldest brother, who was also in the army in France, did visit him in hospital. Many years later, probably about 1960, my wife, Jeff and I located Frank Brooks' grave in a Boulogne cemetery.

My mother-in-law left Edinburgh in 1915 with Eva and went to live with her mother at Newton. Eva's mother realised she must seek some remunerative employment, so, through a married sister at Leicester, she obtained work in a shop there. The war widows' pension was very small – a point on which I have always felt a little bitter. That a man should give his life for his country and his family should only be given a pittance is shameful. Indeed, this has always been so. I have read much of military history and recently read an account of the Peninsular War and how the Duke of Wellington's wounded heroes were treated.

When the war ended Eva and her mother moved to Reading, a position of housekeeper to an army major having been obtained. My wife has spoken a lot about her stay in Reading. She was very happy there. The major with whom they lived had a son and daughter and she was unhappy when they left to come to Lichfield. Her mother had learnt to row and they apparently had some enjoyable times at Caversham on the river.

My wife's parents had been married in 1910 and went to live in Edinburgh – and Evaline Clara Brooks was born on 2 August, 1911. Her father called her the little 'Brooklet'. She has only the vaguest memory of him; her mother, being very reticent, spoke little of him or their married life. It is common courtesy to say, when one or both have passed on, that they were 'happily married', and in the case of my wife's parents the bond of love was very deep. Having heard and read a little of them I am certain I am right in penning these comments.

Uncle Joe, very much like his brother Frank in appearance, is the relative on this side of the family I knew best. I have already related how I stayed with him and Aunt Kit in London in 1931. Uncle Joe was a shrewd and humorous character and a person for whom I had a great fondness. I could write so much of him, but I must curb this desire because the humour of his stories would be lost with reiteration. He left his country cottage home for London when he was thirteen years old. Someone had obtained a job for him at White's Club in the West End. He took up his position of 'buttons' and he told me he had one half-day off every seven days. He spent the first few half-holidays discovering the way to Paddington Station. This was in preparation for his holiday at the end of twelve months, to avoid missing the train on that eventful day to come. What faith, what tenacity of purpose!

He graduated to footman and then butler with some very distinguished families including the Duke of Westminster, the

Wyndham family and Lord Leconfield. He was, over the years, valet to several notable men and there are very few great houses which he did not visit in the course of his duties. He told me that when one of these distinguished families moved from one big house to another, as the social season demanded, a whole train would be requisitioned including coaches and goods wagons. Coaches and horses were transported, to say nothing of household necessities, and probably fifty servants.

I have read many biographies and could relate incidents of which I had read. Uncle Joe was often able to tell me that he had witnessed such events as Lady Margot Asquith falling off a horse at Lord Rosebery's house. Uncle Joe was butler with Lord and Lady Leconfield for many years and when they died he retired in 1939. Retired in this instance is a misnomer. In fact he bought a small farm in Shropshire at a place called Picklescott. I will revert to this later and shall have much to say of the happy holidays we spent there.

Chapter Seven

Eva and I were married on 7 July, 1934, at St Michael's, Lichfield. It was a glorious summer's day with not a cloud in the sky. We held the reception at Trent Valley Hotel and then left for Torquay. It was a long train journey but we were so happy – we had tea on the train and at every station stop we obtained the latest England/Australia cricket Test score. We stayed at a very nice place – the cooking and comfort being first class – we actually stayed at Babbacombe, a delightful place with cliffs and sandy coves. While there, we made friends with Ciss and Cyril, a couple about our age. They possessed a Jowett car, a very roomy tourer of doubtful age but with a stout engine. They took us out every day, touring Devon. We liked Dartmoor and had a few delightful picnics there.

In our family album we have some snaps of this holiday. One of these is of the entrance to the prison; the photo clearly showing a notice forbidding photography. Devon is a beautiful county and our memories of those strawberry and clotted cream teas remain with us. One day we stopped at a country house for such fare and were enjoying our strawberries sitting at a small garden table on a sloping lawn, when quite suddenly Ciss' chair overbalanced and she completely somersaulted, with feet in the air and strawberries all over the place.

We kept up this friendship for many years and in 1936 we arranged to go away together. Eva and I met Ciss and Cyril in London where they picked us up at Uncle Joe's house. We made the journey to Bude the first day and, apart from requiring one new tyre, it was a delightful run, with the map on my knee and smoking my pipe very contentedly. I started smoking a pipe at age 17 and have never stopped.

During this holiday we put up at different places each night and Cyril and I shared the day's expenses. Motoring in 1936

Eva and William (Bill) Barnes on their wedding day, 7th July 1934

was quite different to today, but I am sure that many young people have false ideas of the changes over the years. If we start to record the changes each decade, from 1910, it becomes easier to put things into perspective. I realise that motoring started before 1910 – indeed, Uncle Joe told me that his boss owned one of the six or so cars at the Derby in 1890. In 1910, a few vehicles were about and self-starters had just been introduced. Running-boards were on all cars and the vehicles were roomy. Necessity being the mother of invention, the war had brought about great changes, and by 1920 Ford cars from America were on our roads. They were almost exclusively 'Tin Lizzies', the basis of the Ford fortune. It had a most peculiar transmission with, I believe, two gears. By 1930, William Morris, later Lord Nuffield, was the big name in the British motor industry and the 'Bullnose Morris' was the most popular car. A driver was judged as to his efficiency by how well he could change gears; one had to double de-clutch. Synchromesh had not been introduced and when it was, only first gear was synchro for some years.

Car design improved rapidly in the thirties, the 'Bullnose' having gone out of production about 1929. I bought my first car in 1938, a Morris Eight Saloon – it was twelve months old when I bought it for £75. We kept it until about 1946 when I sold it for £270 and then bought a Standard '8' for £450. I am no mechanic and apart from changing a wheel or spark-plug I leave most other matters to the garage professionals. Since my first car, I now find I have so far owned a total of fourteen different motors and my present 1,500 c.c. Triumph I consider the best I have had. It is very comfortable and will do eighty m.p.h. We have fun asking grandson Peter, two and a half years old at the time of writing, to find the car when we leave it in a car park – he never fails.

After we were married we seemed to have one constant apprehension, the possibility of another war. The 1920s and 1930s were quite troublesome times with great unemployment, strikes and international uncertainty. Hitler, that detestable

German, appeared on the international scene, then Mussolini attacked Ethiopia. Japan attacked China and everyone, I think, realised that another World War was looming. We can, of course, be accused of meeting our troubles half-way. We looked ahead and did not live for the day.

We loved our new house and Eva kept it like the proverbial palace. That first summer was a beauty and the garden was baked hard; so much so that I recall using a coal pick to set a rose bush we had brought from Lichfield, and it lived for years. I worked long hours and went out almost every night after tea; it was in the evenings one could meet the husbands and write new business. Eva always had something nice for supper: indeed, I have always known how fortunate I have been, but looking back now over forty years of married life I would like to record what a wonderful partner I have.

Uncle Joe and Aunt Kit came to see us one Sunday. He had not been able to attend our wedding and I instinctively knew he wanted to know how we were doing. We had a nice day: they came, saw – and went away happy. Uncle Joe had been the last relative to see Eva's father and he felt responsible for her to some extent. Aunt Kit told me some time later that he was pleased and actually made the remark 'Those two have got their heads screwed on'.

A short time before we were married I saw Uncle Fred again. He was still in the army and at that time had the rank of major. They were living at that period in Preston in Lancashire. He was going by road to see his father and step-mother and apparently asked my parents if he should pick them up. He did, and they came through Coventry to see me. I took them up to our nearly completed new house. Uncle Fred was very outspoken and he told a decorator working in the house that his wood graining was poor and in the hall downstairs he said to me 'You won't have much room for a pram here, Bill'. How little we realised then what a bashing that hall would take in the bombing of 1940.

Our social life was mostly with Pru friends and Eva settled happily in Coventry. In 1935 King George Fifth and the country celebrated the Silver Jubilee. About a dozen or so young Pru people decided to make a day of it as it was a Bank Holiday. Our friends with cars took those without their own transport. One young agent named Dill Stovin was a great character; he was not married at this time but was courting a school-teacher from Wolverhampton and I understand that he wrote to her every day. Stovin owned a two-seater open sports car and he asked me to ride with him. Eva was in another car. Dill Stovin was fortunate enough to have 'well-off' parents, but he himself was always most generous. Eva and I referred to him as 'Bulldog Drummond', he was big, strong and full of charm and liked his pint of ale. We all set off for Stratford-on-Avon and hired boats on the river. The girls had each packed a picnic lunch and we partook of this on the banks of the Avon in glorious sunshine. We went further down into Worcestershire. I forget where we had tea, but I do recall stopping at the Red Lion Hotel in Bidford-on-Avon on our way home.

I realised before we were married, that one problem that had to be resolved was what Eva's mother would do. She said she would not live with us, and without her daughter's income she could not live alone, her army pension being a miserable one pound seventy-five pence weekly. Fortunately, we found a happy way out. I called on a Mr Pratt who was works engineer at the Alvis Company and, quite fortuitously, he mentioned how difficult it was to get a good housekeeper. When I told him I could help him he was very interested. The outcome was that Mrs Brooks became his housekeepr and she stayed with him and his son Arthur for some years. This arrangement begat another one. Mrs Brooks' youngest sister Helen was married to Arthur Talbot and they were living at Great Haywood in Staffordshire. Unfortunately he was often out of work owing to the industrial stagnation of the country.

Eva's mother asked Mr Pratt if he could find Arthur Talbot a job at the Alvis. He did so, and we had Arthur staying with us for a couple of weeks until they got fixed up with accommodation. Uncle Arthur and Aunt Nell spent the rest of their lives in Coventry. They liked the place, made countless friends and were happy. Arthur was a born humorist and one of the most popular men I have known. He had volunteered for service at the outbreak of war in 1914 and went through the Gallipoli campaign, but later was badly wounded at the Battle of the Somme in France. He recovered and seemed little the worse for his war experiences when I knew him.

Our married life progressed very happily, and financially I was doing quite well. In the twenty months or so that I was with the Company before we were married, I saved nearly £200 and my total cash on marriage was £250, and Eva had over £100, and so by the standard of those days we had a good start and I told Eva we would have bought the house by the time I was forty-four years old, but we actually paid it off when I was forty-two.

I am aware that I have said nothing about my experiences as a motor cyclist and maybe my grandsons, who I hope may one day read this, would like to hear a little of motor cycling in 1930. So, back to 1930. You will recall that my first job in Coventry was in a shop and each weekend I travelled to Lichfield by train. There would be several benefits, I figured, if I acquired a motorbike. The manager of our shop recommended a small garage to me and I went to inspect a Francis Barnett. These bikes were very popular at that time but have long become extinct. Without any knowledge of the machine, I bought it for £15. I pushed it half-way to my digs, which were at 115 Beresford Avenue, Foleshill. When I came to a quiet part I thought it was time it carried me instead of being pushed, so I propped it up, to have a good look, under a street lamp. It was then I discovered it had no chain. Well, I was certain it had one when I left the garage, so I left the bike there and walked back along the road and within about fifty yards found my chain stretched out like a snake. I arrived at 115 in due course, hot and tired. My landlady, Mrs Fretwell, and her husband Ralph were always wonderful to me and they would be about fifteen years older than me. They wanted to know all about my new purchase and Mrs F couldn't stop laughing and in the end threw her arms around me and said, 'You are a funny lad'.

The following evening Ralph worked on my Fanny Barnett, got it going and showed me how to ride, and from then on I went home each weekend by road and in the summertime I went home on Thursdays, our early-closing day. Eva was never very keen to ride pillion with me but went on a few rides. One Sunday we went to visit Aunt Nell and Uncle Arthur. I recall the event because we nearly met our 'Waterloo': taking a bend in the road too quickly; we almost came off the bike and this frightened us considerably. On another occasion I took Eva to see an uncle and aunt at Newton Regis. On our way back my rear tyre burst but we stayed on and glided into the grass verge without any personal damage. Another time I took Eva's mother to Newton and she quite enjoyed it.

Motor cycling at best is a hazardous business. Returning to Coventry one Monday morning, turning left, as one must at the Stonebridge crossroad, I skidded and the bike slid one way and I careered in the opposite and an Austin Seven car drove straight between us. When I later became unemployed I sold the bike for £5 which would mean that I had had it eighteen months or so.

By 1935 we began hoping for a family but were disappointed. About eighteen months after we were married I asked my mother what she might think if we adopted a baby. She nearly jumped down my throat and told me we hadn't been married five and twenty minutes. It would be about a year later that we knew we were expectant parents. My parents were delighted, but Eva's mother was very quiet about the coming event. We knew she was concerned for her daughter. The summer of 1937 was very good and Eva found the heat rather trying. Our doctor told us the child would be born on 28 August: this day dawned and declined and nothing happened. We were so ignorant of these things, we thought something had gone wrong. On Wednesday, 1 September, Eva asked to be taken into the Highlands Nursing Home. We had decided that if it was a girl we would name her Pamela, but if a boy, we were not sure of a name. The nursing home was a very nice one in a big walled garden in St Nicholas Street. In 1940 it was completely destroyed by German bombing. I kept ringing the nursing home and calling in but nothing happened on Wednesday or Thursday. Rising early on Friday I rang at six-thirty a.m. and was told to ring again at eight-thirty a.m. and when I did so they told me I had a son and both were OK, and so to the nursing home my footsteps took me.

To experience the first thrill of being a parent, only parents can know. I found Eva very happy but very tired and our little cherub superb and so very like his mother in appearance. It required an effort to drag myself away. The nursing staff agreeing, and my work permitting, I was calling in whenever possible. The first person to be informed was naturally 'Nanna Brooks' as she came to be known, my mother-in-law. When she was told about the birth she fainted in my arms. I placed her in a chair and tried to find something to give her but in my distress I gave her cooking sherry, as I later learned, but it did the trick.

Eva came home after ten days, and our life style altered perceptibly. We chose Jeffery William for our son's name; Eva wanted the name spelt as for Jeffery Farnol, the author, and I thoroughly agreed. A number of our Pru friends always referred to Jeffery as 'Little Bill' and John Coltman sometimes still does, despite the fact that Jeff is several inches taller and a stone or two heavier than John or I.

About this time the IRA bombings started in Coventry. We often lay in bed at night and heard the explosions which were always in the town about two miles distant. The fear of war did not abate and the tenor of the news was, 'will Hitler attack or not?' Our defences and military preparedness had been run down to a very low ebb. Undoubtedly the National Government were culpable in this respect. This government was seventy-five per cent Conservative but, I believe, very poorly led. The opposition socialists were such a mixed crew. They played a complete dog in a manger attitude, and opposed rearmament until 1939 and then blamed the government for the poor state of preparedness when war came. You may or may not gather from the above the political persuasion of the writer. I will not leave you in any doubt, as I have never had any myself – Tory is what I have always voted. Recently my thoughts ran to this subject and I tried mentally to find a socialist in my family or in my wife's and I could not, as far as I can ascertain they all vote Conservative. The social spectrum of our families is very wide; from farm labourer on both sides to a British Ambassador. The immediate international concern came to a head after Neville Chamberlain became Premier. He went to see Hitler at Berchtesgaden and then a second visit, to Munich, together with other heads of Government including the French Premier M Daladier. Chamberlain's return from Munich has been written about and commented on endlessly. Sufficient here for me to recount the day as I saw it.

The time was October 1938 and after lunch Eva took Jeff in his pram to visit Gwen Coltman, about twenty minutes' walking distance from Sadler Road, leaving me at home to do my Pru writing. Later in the afternoon I turned the radio on to hear if there was any fresh news when I was staggered and delighted to hear 'It is peace in our time', Chamberlain's remark when he stepped off the plane. All I could think of was dashing off and telling Eva, so I jumped on my bike and pedalled as hard as I could go and was quite out of breath when I got to Coltmans'. John opened the door and in I went spluttering the news and I recall he said 'What's the matter' and I said 'It's p-p-peace in – in our time' and John said, half-laughing, 'Sit down and tell us' and so I did and we were happy and relieved. Trenches were being dug at the time on all available waste land as shelter against possible bombing and so it can be imagined the relief we felt.

We had often thought of buying a car and, in view of the good news, decided to get one. I approached this particular purchase differently to the motor cycle episode. A friend of ours worked at the Parkside Garage and I asked him to look out for a suitable motor. After a few days he called to tell me they had a nice Morris Eight saloon, the registration number of which I shall never forget, CHP 332. At this time, I had only driven two different cars for a total distance of about five miles so that when I collected our Morris I had to declare my inexperience and ask for someone to drive me home or give me a brief lesson. This the garage did and I drove as far as Fillongley village on the north side of the city.

We had already had a garage built by a friend but it was most awkward to drive in and out of, so the garage man put the car away. Eva and I discussed where we should go for our first ride and decided we should go to Lichfield on Sunday. To say that I was confident at the prospect would be quite untrue, but Eva had no qualms. We set off with Jeffery asleep on the back seat and reached Lichfield without mishap. I recall that my biggest worry seemed to be overtaking cycling clubs. It was a common sight to see twenty to forty men and girls on racing cycles in the 1930s.

I suppose the one place that has given us more pleasure than any other in visiting is the village of King's Cliffe, in Northamptonshire. Eva's Aunt Edie and Uncle Herbert lived there and our first visit I recall was by train, after we were married and before Jeff came. Many Northamptonshire villages are very like Cotswold villages with their stone buildings. We arrived at Cliffe one Saturday and, as Eva had predicted, Aunt Edie and Uncle Herbert were at the station to meet us. They were a truly wonderful couple. Uncle was self-employed as a collyweston slater, very outspoken and with a rustic humour which I appreciated. Aunt Edie was a wonderful cook, but each Sunday the beef joint was cooked at the village bakehouse. The mixture for the Yorkshire pudding was taken to the baker in a separate vessel and the baker poured it into the pan at the right time. The joint, which I believe was often the H-bone, rested on a tripod in the tray and the Yorkshire pud got the dripping from the meat. Many villagers took advantage of the hot oven and I can say that I have never tasted better cooking before or since.

With the acquisition of the car we went to Cliffe on Whit Sunday 1939, this being our longest run to date. Aunt Edie and Uncle Herbert had one daughter only, Marjorie, who married Ray Woolley about 1930. At the time of our visit in 1939 Ray and Marjorie were staying at Cliffe and our visit was a happy one. They asked us to go back the next day and take Eva's mother, which we did. It was almost a ritual at Cliffe to gather primroses in the meadows and woods. Most of the land around formed part of the Marquis of Exeter's estate, the family seat being Burghley House. I suppose, over the last forty odd years there have been only one or two years, excluding the war years, when we have not visited Cliffe.

While we were at Cliffe in 1939 Marjorie and Ray asked us to visit them at their home outside Bradford, which we did in August. This of course was prior to the building of the motor roads. I studied the map and wrote out my route. We stopped at Sheffield for lunch, and Jeffery was much admired when he got down from the table and walked up to the orchestra. We reached Saltaire in good time and were made very welcome by Ray and Marjorie who had two children, Gerald and Barbara, aged about seven and four at that time and today forty-six and forty-three respectively, and both married.

This was a very happy holiday. Ray showed us local beauty spots and he and I walked across Ilkley Moor. Our time was so full during this week that we did not read a paper and when we arrived back at Coventry we were amazed to read how much the international scene had deteriorated and war, we knew, was only just a matter of time.

Chapter Eight

Sunday, 3 September 1939 was the fateful day when war was declared and this was Jeffery's second birthday. Eva arranged a nice birthday tea and Aunt Nell and Uncle Arthur and their son Bill came. After tea we went into the garden to watch Jeffery trying to ride his new little tricycle. We then saw the barrage balloons going up all around us and our hearts sank. Readers of history will know that the following six-month period is known as the 'phoney war' – nothing happened. I suppose we were lulled into a false sense of security. My mother and father came for a weekend visit, which, of course, I would not have agreed to had there been any bombing of Coventry at that time.

Some months prior to the declaration of war, I had been recommended for promotion. My interview with the Divisional Manager took place at our Coventry office. The manager's name was Anderson. A big Scot, he said he would test my knowledge of the business, and so plied me with questions: all went well until he asked me a question regarding a man claiming on behalf of an employed chauffeur, but fortunately for me the phone rang and I promptly said 'Shall I leave, sir' and he said that I should. I dived, or rather my hand did, into a cupboard in the outer office and I found the information to answer the question. When I heard the phone put down I went back and the interview proceeded satisfactorily, and promotion was offered.

I was asked the type of work I would prefer to become involved in, selling or administration. The former appealed to me and this seemed to please Mr Anderson. Sometime later, the Company informed me of my promotion date and also said I should work our Leamington district and also Stratford-on-Avon. These districts covered a very large area, several hundred square miles in fact, and some nights I had to stay away from home. This aspect got much worse with the coming of war and petrol rationing. It was not long before I began to wonder whether I had made a mistake in accepting promotion. Petrol rationing was quite severe. The domestic allowance was I believe one and a half gallons per week and my business ration soon came down to two gallons which was quite hopeless – if I couldn't travel I could not write business or get home. My expense allowance was meagre but I could charge hotel expenses.

My experiences became very weird during this period of trying to get petrol without coupons and travelling in the blackout. Vehicle lighting restrictions were very tight. Sidelights had to be reduced so that light was emitted through an area of one-inch diameter, the near-side headlight bulb removed and the other headlight had to be masked. The available light one had to drive with was abysmal and to exceed twenty miles per hour was definitely dangerous. Farmers were the best source of illegal petrol supplies, but I relied on the district agents, with whom I worked, to see me right. I got quite adept at siphoning petrol from cans and always carried a piece of rubber hose and of necessity often tasted petrol in my mouth. Sometimes an agent would inform me that he had a can of petrol in a certain country lane. I recall a publican having a five-gallon can in a small shed in a field some way from the pub: this was in the fruit-growing district of Worcestershire. The publican would not accompany me and he informed me that if the police came and caught me he would disclaim any knowledge. It was quite a serious offence to obtain petrol without a coupon, hence the publican's attitude.

The position was a ridiculous one: I, like many other people, was trying to do a job without the means. Fuel had to be rationed, but business life had to go on and the two claims were incompatible. The most audacious case of corrupt practice was a police sergeant who left a five-gallon drum for me in a certain hedge. The policeman is now dead and so are most of the other people who helped me illegally. I was very grateful to them and would add that they did not do it for personal profit as I seldom paid over the normal price.

To say that life at this time was difficult is to put it mildly. The winter of 1940 was a bad one and added to our troubles. One could not obtain anti-freeze liquid and one morning I was on my way to Evesham, having stayed the previous night in Stratford, when clouds of steam came from the engine and I realised I was frozen up. The roads were snowbound and frozen but a lady motorist stopped and took me on to Evesham. I arranged with a garage at Stratford to collect and repair my car. Two days later, and due to go home, a colleague Geoff Parmley, who was in Evesham, took me in his car back to Stratford. I found my car left outside the garage but to my horror it registered very little petrol in the tank and the garage closed with no-one about. When I informed Geoff of my position he said he would travel behind me as he lived at Kenilworth, only five miles short of Coventry. We waved goodnight but I was only on the outskirts of Kenilworth when my car packed up and yours truly was in the soup. I found a small pub open, but all they could do was to direct me to the nearest garage which was at Crackley, about a mile or so away. The garage was closed but I knocked up the proprietor, who was in bed. He swore, but provided me with a can of petrol. I reached home at about eleven p.m. and Eva was quite worried.

All men aged between eighteen and forty-five years had to register for military service on given dates; my date I believe was in July 1940. The day I registered we went on to Picklescott for a week's holiday on Uncle Joe's farm. I have already written of Uncle Joe and Aunt Kit. In 1939 Lady Leconfield died and Uncle retired – and achieved a life-long ambition of owning a farm, having bought Top House Farm at Picklescott. It was only thirty acres but was a lovely old house. The peace and quietness of the country was beautiful and we enjoyed that week. I will have more to say about Picklescott when we had further holidays there after the war ended.

The phoney war period ended with the coming of spring

1940, when Germany attacked and drove us out of France and forced an armistice with the French, and then we had to suffer the bombing raids. If anyone tells me that they have been in a bombing raid and were not scared I just don't believe them. The first time the sirens sounded was in the night. Eva shook me, as I was well asleep, and then I heard 'they are here'. We rose quickly, Eva asked me to carry Jeffery downstairs so I went to his cot and caught hold of him, and all the cot clothes I could manage. Something went bump, bump on the handrail going downstairs and I realised it was Jeff's head. We went under the stairs and when the sirens stopped howling it went deathly quiet and then we heard the toilet being flushed next door. After half an hour or so the 'all clear' sounded and so we went back to bed. We learned later that no German plane got as far as Coventry, but bombs had been dropped on Pailton, a village about eight miles away.

After this, the raids became many and often, and for weeks we never slept with our clothes off, and soon we had our bed downstairs. The noise during an air raid is awful: apart from the high-pitched whistle as bombs fall and the explosions, and guns roaring, there is the rattle of everything which is loose such as doors, windows and trellis-work in the garden. We had an Anderson shelter which we shared with Mr and Mrs Jones, our next door neighbours, but more often than not we stayed under the stairs because of Jeff's bronchitis.

To relate all the hair-raising nights we had would take me too long, but one or two may be worth recording. We were under the stairs one night which was reasonably quiet, when we heard a low-flying plane approaching; there was no ack-ack response and we thought it must be one of ours, when a stick of bombs was released. Two bombs fell in Wallace Road, just to the back of us, one being a direct hit on a shelter, killing a family we knew well. Fortunately, the other bombs fell on an allotment in our street. It was quiet immediately afterwards and I went into the front garden to see what damage was visible. Mr and Mrs Jones had done likewise and the sight presented by our neighbours was quite comical: Mr Jones in his long johns and Mrs Jones half-undressed in the moonlight.

During the Battle of Britain, of which we saw nothing, the news of high enemy plane losses was the talk of everyone; the radio gave each side's losses frequently and it sounded to us like a cricket score.

About this time we went to King's Cliffe for a weekend. When stopping at a garage for petrol another motorist told me he had just been machine-gunned.

I left Eva and Jeff at Cliffe when I returned to Coventry on the Sunday night. Having just got the car into the garage the sirens sounded. Mr Jones was on his own too, he went to the shelter and I joined him. It was only a small raid but one bomb dropped fairly near to us. This was the only time I heard Ern Jones swear, when in the solitude of the shelter he said 'the blasted buggers'.

Another night we had taken shelter but nothing happened and when the 'all clear' sounded Mr and Mrs Jones came running out; she was shouting 'come on Ern, come on Ern'. These neighbours, to whom I have referred several times, were, in 1940, about fifty years of age. They had two sons, Ron and Derek, grand lads who would put many present young people to shame. At the outbreak of war they joined up together with all the members of their rugger club. Ron was a BA of outstanding intelligence and appearance. Alas, Derek was an also-ran in academic achievements, but a most likeable lad. Our neighbours on the other side were of our own age group. They had a baby son, born some weeks before ours. When Ron and Derek came home each day, when the babies were small, they used to count the nappies on the lines and shout to their mother 'Jeff's winning' or 'Colin's winning'.

Ron and Derek were soon in France, they had joined the 7th Batt. Warwickshire Regiment. At the time of Dunkirk Mrs Jones was very upset – would she ever see her boys again? I well remember listening to the radio news at this time and it was announced that evacuation of British and Allied troops would cease at the weekend. When Saturday came and she had still not heard we were very perturbed. After lunch Eva suggested that we take Mr and Mrs Jones out in the car. We did so and had a picnic tea in the country. Mrs Jones played with Jeff but it was obvious to each of us we were putting on a show. We did not stay long and soon came back home. Within a few minutes Mrs Jones came running into our house shouting 'They are back and safe'; she was almost hysterical with delight having received a telegram to let her know they were safe.

Rationing of foodstuffs and other things was now becoming much tighter and life generally more difficult. The decrease in daylight hours saw an increase in enemy bombing, so much so that I could not see any point in staying, as I was not working in Coventry. During one heavy raid whilst under the stairs, I said to Eva 'If we are still alive in the morning I shall take you to Lichfield' and she readily agreed. We parked ourselves on my parents for a couple of weeks or so. After this move I stayed most nights wherever I was working and my experiences were many and varied.

The Company changed my districts of activity quite frequently and I worked in Birmingham, Rugby, Worcester, Nuneaton, Tamworth and others. Hotel accommodation was difficult to obtain for a variety of reasons and so agents often put me up on improvised beds, because few people went upstairs to sleep now.

I remember staying one night with Freddy Harris and his wife at Nuneaton. We were sitting round the fire talking when the air raid siren sounded, but we thought this was probably another raid on Coventry, some eight miles away. Fred was a little deaf, but I heard a plane coming closer. Mrs Harris picked up their baby and suggested going under the stairs when the 'ack-ack' started up. Then the bombs were dropped and one must have been very close because the debris falling on the roof of the house was quite deafening. When things quietened down we heard knocking on the wall from next door: the occupants, I was told, were two ladies. Fred and I went to find what they wanted and were told that they thought an unexploded bomb had fallen in the garden. We searched carefully for some time but could not find any evidence, and so tried to reassure them. We eventually went to bed and next morning found very little damage to the house.

I went into our Nuneaton office a day or two after this and the District Manager (DM) asked me if I was interested in renting a house in Nuneaton. I quickly obtained the address of the house in question and dashed off, but as I left him, the DM said he had already told Mr Bradford and Mr Coltman, the General Branch and Ordinary Branch reps. I beat them to it and secured the house. They both lived in Coventry and were as anxious as I was to move out.

We arranged for our furniture etc, to be moved on 15 November, 1940: this date is indelibly impressed on my mind because of the big raid on Coventry on the 14th, which stopped our removal on the arranged day.

I was at Lichfield this particular night, so that I could bring Eva back with me to facilitate the move. The sirens went quite early in the evening and we heard gunfire in the distance. It was not until next morning that we knew that a heavy raid had taken place on a Midlands town and we guessed it might be Coventry. We left Lichfield for Coventry hoping we could be moved. The police were stopping all traffic entering Coventry unless you lived there. Police were stopping traffic every few miles in fact, but eventually we reached our house in Sadler Road. It was still standing but the windows were broken and the front door had been blown off. We discovered that an old friend had arrived before us. This was Cliff Small, an old schoolfriend, and now an agent with the Company at Lutterworth. He had nailed the door on and left a note pinned to it.

We did not waste time, however, at Sadler Road because we were anxious to discover how Nanna Brooks had fared. The journey from Sadler Road to Caldicote Road, about a mile and a half, was most tortuous. Rubble and wreckage of all sorts blocked the roads and our local church was completely demolished. Nothing had been cleared and our passage was difficult trying to drive through bricks and sandstone, lamp-posts and telegraph poles. We did make it to the top of Middlemarch Road, named after George Eliot's book. I left the car at this point and went alone to find if Eva's mother was alright or not. I opened the back door and she greeted me as unconcerned as ever – they had been in the shelter all night. We quickly decided she could not stay there but had to come back with us. She agreed, and packed a case to take with her what was necessary. When driving off from Caldicote Road the police would not allow me to return the way I had come; the road had been closed because of unexploded bombs. Twice more I was stopped and found other roads closed. But I found a way out and we were quite relieved. We then called at the Alvis works to let Mr Pratt know I was taking Mrs Brooks to Lichfield and we also told Uncle Arthur that we would take Aunt Nell and Cousin Bill to Tamworth relatives.

Looking back on this journey I am amazed at the faith I had in my small Morris car of only eight horsepower and described as a four-seater – into which we stowed four adults and two boys of three years and fourteen years, and three suitcases and other clothes. It was so crammed I had difficulty in driving. I was taking Aunt Nell and Bill to relatives at Newton Regis which is about five miles north of Tamworth. To avoid extra mileage I stopped and asked a passing motorist, having explained my position, if they would take Aunt Nell and son to Newton. This they willingly did, and so saved me about ten miles.

We stayed, or rather, Eva, Jeff and Nanna did, at Lichfield for about two weeks and then we arranged for our furniture and effects to be moved to Nuneaton.

Eva's mother was a great help in the move and so we got settled into 206 The Long Shoot. It was very nice to live as a family again. Nuneaton had two sharp air raids after our arrival but nothing more of any consequence.

Passing through Coventry one day soon after the big raid, a policeman was on point duty at the Broadgate crossroads; he stopped my line of traffic and I was close to him. I thought

I recognised him so I wound the car window down and said 'Hello, Tiddly'. He looked at me sharply and said 'Well, I'll be damned'. He had probably never been so addressed since he left school. He was in fact Bill Phillips who I went to school with at Whittington and was always known as 'Tiddly'. We had not met since our school-days. He was in the Staffordshire police and was one of many who had been drafted into Coventry.

The casualties in this one raid were six hundred killed and many more injured. One fire contingent from Stoke-on-Trent was completely wiped out, together with their engine.

One of my many friends in Coventry was Ernest Wilby. He was an agent with the Company. We made it a habit to meet each Thursday morning when paying our accounts into the office and then have a coffee at the Geisha Café in Hertford Street. This was, of course, before I was promoted. Ernest, when so many were being called for service, decided to join the Fire Service. He saw German bombing in plenty and had some hair-raising experiences. We are still good friends and go to visit each other. Ernest and Betty have one son, who obtained a LLB degree at Birmingham University. Since the war we have talked of our experiences during those dreadful war years. The heavy raid on Coventry, 14 November, 1940, saw Ernest Wilby actively engaged. He told me that he was on the flat roof of Lloyds Bank in Broadgate that night and he saw a landmine explode on Broadgate, possibly one hundred yards from the bank. Ernest said it threw him flat on his back but he suffered no injuries. When I later saw the area, the only buildings standing were two banks, Lloyds and National Provincial, as it was then known. The firemen were called in half-way through the night because of a lack of water.

The fire service had to be very mobile, and another experience Ernest related was when on his way to Nuneaton he was blown off the fire-engine just as they were entering Nuneaton, again without injury. He also informed me that he and the fire crew were at different times sent to the London docks and also to Bristol. I have read since the war ended that British

Intelligence broke the German code and so became aware of German intended activity and bombing targets, and so additional fire crews could be despatched to the expected area of military activity.

The enemy, having been held or subdued over Britain, now in June 1941 attacked Russia. This, of course, resulted in a diminution of the bombing of Coventry – so much so that raids were few and far between. The relief was considerable. I can still see the improvised repair work in my mind's eye. Boarded-up windows and waterproof sheets on house roofs. The water mains were laid on the ground and not buried, and the gas mains were also visible above ground. Everything looked terribly drab and nothing could be bought without coupons.

But our personal life improved and we were reasonably happy at The Long Shoot. When working in the country I was occasionally able to buy from farmers such things as eggs or bacon. When one considers how small the ration of food was, such as two ounces of butter per head per week, one egg, four ounces of meat – it can be appreciated how welcome my efforts were. Looking back now my wife wonders however she managed, particularly with Jeff so often ill and she unable to go out and queue for various items.

The house we took at Nuneaton had a large garden and was full of growing cabbage and sprouts. Jeff has never liked such things. I have often wondered if he had a surfeit of these vegetables at that time.

Chapter Nine

I could not understand why I was not called up to the forces because my occupation was not reserved. The war had been going for two years and I had lived with the expectation of being called up. But at last it came, telling me to report to the barracks at Worcester. Until now Eva and I had shared our troubles, being together. Alas, like thousands more we had to part. She was very upset and told me she was sure history would be repeated and that I would not come back, as had happened in the previous generation, early in the Great War. I arrived at Worcester station to be met by army trucks to take us up to Norton Barracks. It was then I learned how the army conveyed troops in lorries, each man standing up and so occupying the minimum of floor space. We soon arrived at the barracks, about two miles' distance away, and then began the documentation process, and so on.

Our first army meal will never be forgotten. Whether it was put on to shock the recipients I shall never know, but I do know I have seen better food fed to pigs. Later we were kitted out and our civilian clothes posted home. The men I was with attracted most of my attention – and a more comprehensive cross-section of humanity it would be difficult to find. We all had to declare our occupation in a loud voice (army fashion). I learned my fellow sufferers were: editor of a daily paper, shop manager, farmer's son, insurance inspector (Farmers' Union), window cleaner, dustman, road-sweeper and professional backer.

When we were in khaki it was difficult for a while to recognise any chap one had previously spoken to. We were formed into platoons of about thirty-five men. Allocated to each platoon there was a sergeant, corporal and lance-corporal. They were very efficient at their job and soon knocked us into shape and in two weeks they considered that we were smart enough to be allowed into town.

The army is a great leveller; it brings out the best in some and the worst in others, I discovered. We had one among us, a big Birmingham chap, who had too much to say for my liking, but events caught up with him. We were paraded one day and marched off with our sergeant grinning broadly. Stopping outside a medical hut, we were soon inside and told to strip to the waist: it was obvious to all that it was a jab parade.

I found from observation that if anything was a little bit unpleasant it was much better to get it over, so I was in the first three to step up for treatment. The doctor jabbed one arm while a medical orderly did the other arm. I looked along the line of bare chests and saw the big Birmingham man fall over in a faint. He was strangely quiet after this episode. Arriving first back in the room where we had left our clothes, I started to dress, but the waiting sergeant said 'Oh no, back through again you go' – and so we did, to have a smallpox vaccination.

The sequel to this jab parade was that we were given thirty-six hours excused duty, but on the Sunday morning, owing to a shortage of troops, we were ordered out of our beds to go on church parade. The sergeant said there would be no inspection so did not need to go to any trouble concerning personal appearance. Alas, this proved to be inaccurate, and I was booked for being unshaven but the charge was dropped. Most of us were 'under the weather' after three injections.

The weather while I was at Norton Barracks was quite good and some of the training I enjoyed, but some I loathed. I have never been interested in fire-arms, and taking a Bren gun to pieces and putting it back together again was purgatory. After a few weeks they took us on the River Severn below Worcester for a little more realistic warplay. We were in flat-bottomed boats, trying to cross the Severn, with thunder-flash fireworks being thrown at us and into the boats. Unfortunately, our boat capsized and two chaps were drowned. We then had to practise funeral marching. That weekend I applied for a forty-eight-hour pass and got it, Eva having written telling me she was going to King's Cliffe to visit Aunt Edie and Uncle Herbert. I was happy beyond words and the pleasure of that weekend I shall never forget. Aunt Edie's cooking, after army food, was out of this world.

Jeffery at this time would have been four years old and very intelligent. I found him somewhat reticent when I was on leave, as though he was aware the pleasure of being together was transitory. I got home as often as I could but I had to leave in the night to avoid the tearful scenes of saying goodbye to Jeff.

After some eighteen weeks at Norton Barracks we were posted to a field battalion. We arrived at Market Rasen in Lincolnshire and were part of the 48th Infantry Division. We were billeted in Nissen huts in a wood or coppice. The food at this unit was quite good; the cookhouse was an old farm building. When the Company Sergeant Major learned that I was in the insurance business he talked to me quite a bit and then gave me a job in Company office. His name was Harry Parry and known to the troops as 'Happy Harry'. He suggested that I be permanent duty clerk and have a camp bed in the office. I agreed and found life there quite pleasant; no muster parade and a leisurely breakfast in the cookhouse of whatever I fancied. I had to stay in the office from seven p.m. to eight a.m., but as we were miles away from any sort of entertainment I was quite happy, warm and comfortable, and just read. There were many phone calls each night, mainly from Battalion HQ. After a few weeks we moved to Marsh Chapel, a tiny village on the coast. It seems a misnomer to say coastline, as anyone familiar with the East Coast knows what an expanse of mud flats there is in certain districts. We were now on coastal defence and we had miles of barbed wire and a few enemy air attacks, but nothing serious.

It was about this time that I became acquainted with John Harman. He was in a different Company of the Battalion and for some reason unknown to me, whether chance or selection, he asked me if I would have a drink with him at the village pub. He was going to treat a group of his colleagues and he said that he would be glad if I went with them. He left money to keep them going all evening, and we soon left them. John Harman was an outstanding chap and most interesting. We must have walked quite a few miles that night around the countryside and probably never met a soul.

John told me that his father was a financier and a former friend of Horatio Bottomley, of infamous memory. Bottomley, for my younger readers, was a quite notorious financier and went to prison for his nefarious activities after the First World War. John's family owned Lundy Island and when on leave he was often late returning because the weather and availability of a boat determined his departure time from the island. I recall that during that walk he told me that he had ideas about the submarine menace and how he could help if only he could talk to Winston Churchill. He said his father could get an interview with the PM but that he would never appeal to his father for help. I never heard any more about this matter, but have never ceased to wonder how a man with such outstanding ability could be occupying a lowly rank in the army. It was several years later that I read in the press that Sgt J Harman had met his death in Malaya. He attacked a machine-gun position and silenced it single-handed, but subsequently died. He was posthumously awarded the Victoria Cross, the highest award for gallantry.

It was also in the press that I read of a memorial being erected to the memory of J Harman on Lundy Island. This island has attracted me from a bird-watching angle many times but alas, we have never been there.

The training began to get tougher in the 8th Battalion and soon we were joining in Divisional schemes. Returning to camp after taking part in a field scheme on a hot day Lt Dickie ordered us to start at the double. I was 'all in' and fell out, and was told to make my own way back to camp and also to report 'sick'. This I did next morning. The MO gave me three days excused duties, but what you are excused from depends on whose authority you are under. I was promptly sent to the cookhouse with several others and in a few hours had peeled three hundredweight of potatoes and two large bags of carrots. The outcome of this affair was quite important to me but not, of course, to the British Army. They sent me to Brace Bridge Hospital for examination where two army doctors examined my feet. One MO was somewhat rude but the other was friendly, and I was given a sealed envelope to take back to my CO. Before leaving the hospital I went into a toilet and opened the envelope to read what they had to say about me. Their remarks were that they recommended medical downgrading to B2 as I was flat-footed. After attending a Medical Board to confirm this, I knew my days at the unit were limited.

Before leaving the subject of this Battalion, I must tell of my only leave while in Lincolnshire. The Battalion moved off to take part in some Divisional exercise and I, with a couple of dozen, were left behind as the rear party. Our corporal in the Company office made me out a pass, but he made me promise that I would be back at 24.00 hours on Sunday. Home was reached but how, I have quite forgotten. The return journey is well remembered. From Nuneaton to Leicester it was by train, but having two hours to wait for a connection, I decided to call on Aunt Pem and Uncle Tom who lived in Derwent Street. Having tea with them almost caused me to miss the train but I jumped on it as it was moving. It was dark when the train drew into Lincoln and after asking for a bus to Market Rasen, I was told that the last bus had gone. This meant that there was no alternative to walking, and just then the air raid siren sounded. Having found the Market Rasen road, the walk began. A bus overtook me but the driver told me he was turning off the road in a mile or so. However, he let me get on for that distance. After several miles I came to an aerodrome and went into the guardroom and asked if they had a truck going my way, but the answer was in the negative. They offered me a cycle if I could return it the next day, but this was impossible, whereupon they gave me a mug of cocoa and bread and cheese.

The distance from Lincoln to Market Rasen is approximately twenty miles but it is rather flat, which helped a little. No one passed me, nor any vehicle, and the only sound was dogs barking as I walked through the villages. My army boots did make a clatter. After a few more miles, feeling tired, I lay down on the gravel path for a while. Eventually I reached the camp and climbed through the hedge and so to the Nissen hut. Next morning the chaps wanted to know what time I had got in. The corporal was glad to see that I was back. Soon after this I learned that they were posting me back to the depot at Worcester.

It was actually 11 November, 1942 when I left the 8th Battalion. The personal equipment that we had to carry now, in retrospect, makes me shudder. My greatcoat was worn and on this sat my webbing belt and shoulder straps with ammunition pouches, side arms, water bottle, valise, haversack, tin hat, rifle and full kitbag and one blanket. An army truck took me to Grimsby railway station and on to a train for Worcester.

When we stopped at Nottingham, we were able to get a cup of tea and in doing so I met Freddy Meek. He was now in the RAF and going on leave. Before being called up he was a Prudential agent at Worcester. I had worked with him and visited his home, so the meeting was welcome for me, and in view of the load I had to carry, quite fortunate. When we reached Worcester it was getting dark. Fred took my kitbag, which was a great help. The stone sets at the station were very uneven and I promptly fell on my back, but no harm done. At the depot I was accommodated for one night and next morning taken to Malvern. Here about sixty or so troops were billeted in a rather nice country house. The ways of the army are very strange, but they must have known what they were doing: my rifle and blanket were taken from me at Worcester and at Malvern I collected new blankets that were very damp from the cellar. This holding unit was so crowded that out buildings were used. The sergeant who was trying to accommodate us was almost in despair. Eventually I came to rest in a stable, and given a camp-bed with only three legs. The stable door was six inches short of meeting the ground and so let in plenty of draught. There was no light in the place and I was the only occupant. One night under these conditions was more than enough and next day I found room for myself in the loft with a number of others.

Life was very flat at this place; no duties, no parades and nowhere to sit. It was so boring that one day I found a broom and swept the leaves up in the drive. We had one officer with us, an elderly captain. When I was sweeping he came and spoke to me and I believe he was as bored as I was. He told me that if I had been there a week earlier I could have gone to Canada guarding prisoners of war. I noticed that he was wearing the MC ribbon on his chest.

Soon after this I was on the move again. A CQMS, another private and myself were posted to Prestatyn in North Wales. The camp, when we reached it, was a good set-up. We were told it was a former holiday camp but many army huts had been added. It was, in fact, No. 6 Primary Training Centre and about six hundred new recruits came in each month. I was put to work in the Pay Office and was quite delighted to be doing something intelligent and useful at last. The Company Quartermaster Sergeant (CQMS) I had come up with from Malvern was put in charge of our office. I read up all I could on army pay matters and was made a company pay clerk. Life was very pleasant at Prestatyn; no air raids, good food and many physical comforts.

The possibility of getting Eva and Jeffery up to live at Prestatyn began to dawn on me. Having obtained Eva's willingness, indeed joy, at the prospect, I made the necessary application. Having obtained this, my next problem was to find suitable accommodation for the three of us. In this I was lucky. How I got in touch with the lady, my memory fails me. She was the widow of an army officer who had a quite beautiful bungalow. We agreed terms but they included the proviso that I help in the garden.

Eva and Jeffery came to Prestatyn and my wife has said that the months spent there were some of the happiest of our married life. The living out allowance was given, and enabled us to live quite comfortably with our other income. Unfortunately Jeffery Bill caught measles the second day at Prestatyn, but he soon recovered.

At this time all recruits had to be informed of their monetary entitlements and to this end, in our camp, a man from our office gave each intake of troops a talk. When he was posted to another camp some other person had to be found to give the talk. Imagine my surprise when the CQMS chief clerk informed me that the Commanding Officer (CO) wanted me to give the talk. He requested that I write out what I intended to say, and the CO would approve it or otherwise. That evening I wrote out several sheets and next day the CO gave his OK.

The general idea was to speak for half an hour or more and then invite questions. From the queries which the men normally brought into the office, it was not difficult to guess the questions that were likely to be put to me. It was arranged that one hundred and fifty chaps should be at each session. The NCOs marched them into an army hut and I stood on the stage. An officer sat at the back of the men and I realised that my performance would be reported: all went well and I coped with the questions.

It was the normal pattern to get a number of questions on income tax – some quite simple but some I had to defer for lack of detail. This job continued, with my quite enjoying it, until the camp closed later that year.

After a while Mrs Young, our landlady, became difficult. I believe she thought I wasn't doing enough in the garden so we obtained alternative accommodation with a Mrs Cooper in Meliden village. She proved a great friend, and she really loved Jeffery and life was very pleasant.

We clerks all took turns to be duty clerk and the time came round about every ten days. When my turn came I had to stay at camp all night. Living out, as I was now doing, I could not have any meals in camp but following night duty I was allowed my breakfast.

Bill Barnes in the army, 1943

The summer of 1943 was quite good and encouraged us to explore the countryside which, inland from Prestatyn, is quite beautiful. Eva's mother came to Prestatyn for a few days and we found her accommodation in the avenue that we were living in. She was happy to see us again, and we to see her, but more especially she was happy to be with Jeff. My parents also came up for a few days and quite enjoyed their holiday. In both cases we took our visitors around and I recall having tea on the sand dunes. Eva, Jeff and I found some beautiful walks over the hills south of Meliden and we used to sit in rocky coves which formed a delightful suntrap, and look out over the countryside to sea.

It was in the summer of 1943 after our forces had captured Sicily that the Italians asked for peace terms and everyone thought the end of the war was in sight, but, alas, it lasted another two years. This same summer must have been good – the time just flew and we were very content.

The quiet of Prestatyn was shattered one night however

when a mine was washed onto the beach and exploded. It made a rare bang.

We eventually received our last intake of recruits at the camp and were informed that we should be posted. But first we had to take a test, and were graded educationally. It occurred to me that a better posting ought to be obtained if one did well in the test, so the old 'grey matter' was stirred a bit. I tried quite hard and did pretty well. The following day we were interviewed. The officer that I saw was very open and the first thing he said to me was 'what are you doing in the infantry?' I told him he could probably answer that better than I could. He was very agreeable and said he would see I had a good posting. We were coming to the end of another happy period and Eva asked a lot of questions as to where I thought I might be going, but I knew no more than she did.

In due course we were informed of our different postings and I, and several others, were being posted to Aldershot. This place is often thought of as the HQ of the British Army and it is certainly a great army centre, with many different Barracks. It was a lovely warm day in August when I left Prestatyn with several more chaps, and Eva and Jeff were left down in the dumps.

Chapter Ten

The memory of this move is very clear because we had to stand in the train nearly all the way. On arriving at Aldershot we were quickly subjected to a discipline unknown at Prestatyn. Many more troops arrived at Buller Barracks with us, it was like joining the army again, with all the instructions and shouting of Sergeant Majors. They eventually got us sorted and allocated to different barrack rooms. It was during this sorting out that I met Jimmy Brown, and formed a lasting friendship. He told me he was from Edinburgh and worked for the General Accident Insurance Co. He was tall, dark and quite well educated, with a sense of fun, and proved to be a very good friend, as I shall later relate.

We were all transferred to the Royal Army Service Corps and before anything else was done with us, new cap badges and shoulder flashes were issued and worn. The RASC, as the name implies, provides all the services to the army such as clerks, shorthand writers, bakers, drivers and many more trades. We learned that we were to start on a 'course'. The more intelligent were to commence on a staff duties and shorthand course, the next in order of their assessment of intellect were to be clerks and the remainder were destined to be storemen. Jimmy and I were delighted to be together on staff duties.

We were instructed and lectured by Army Education Corps personnel. We were provided with normal writing necessities and a good blank notebook. The system of imparting knowledge to us was, as I understand it, similar to university lectures. There were few interruptions and we all listened carefully. It was quite an asset to be able to write quickly. Many men, I am sure, spend a lifetime in the army without ever really understanding how it ticks. This course, if we did well enough to gain a pass mark, was intended to equip us to hold any clerical job from the War Office down to Brigade HQ. To be able to assess the importance of any written message and to forward it along the correct lines of communication – must sound very simple to my readers, but I can assure you, the reverse is true. It appeared to me, and I think to the others in the class, that the course was most absorbing and everyone seemed keen to learn.

Eva and Jeffery stayed at Prestatyn for two months or so, and in one of her letters she told me that Jeff was to have his tonsils removed and was going into Chester Hospital. This was worrying for Eva, but all ended well. Eva had apparently written and told Aunt Kit and Uncle Joe that I had been posted to Aldershot and in her reply Aunt Kit had informed Eva that there was a plaque in the Garrison Church at Aldershot in memory of her brother. Aunt Kit had previously told us the sad story: her brother, Sergeant Clark, with his troop was apparently exercising on some beach in England with their horses. Two of the men got into difficulties in the water and Sergeant Clark tried to rescue them, but alas he was washed out to sea and lost.

The next Sunday I was on church parade – and at Aldershot it really was some parade. It appeared to me as if they were trying to retain some of the pageantry of the pre-war days. The RASC band was at the head of my column and I must say that I felt quite proud marching along to the strains of martial music. We arrived at the church, which was a red brick building with ivy or similar creeper growing up the walls. We filed into church which was literally packed. I gazed round the church and you will appreciate my surprise when I saw a stone tablet set into the wall, adjacent to where I was seated, which read 'To the memory of Sergeant Clark' etc. Aunt Kit was delighted when I later told her.

Speaking of marching with the band reminds me of an episode I would like to relate. It concerns my stay at Norton Barracks while doing our initial training. We left the barracks one Friday morning to march to a firing-range some fifteen miles away. It was a nice morning and we were soon told to march at ease, and I would add it is very difficult to march out of step, we could carry our rifle how we liked and whistle or sing. Every fifty minutes a whistle was blown to indicate five or maybe ten minutes' rest. We soon stretched ourselves out and endeavoured to raise our feet above the horizontal.

Having reached the firing range we each had to fire a given number of rounds and some of those men not firing would lie in the Butts, that is, in a trench below the targets, to replace them as required. I found this job interesting, and uncanny hearing the lead shot arriving two feet or so above, overhead.

When the firing was finished we made camp in a wood and had something to eat. We were then told that we were to be attacked after dark by troops from another unit. We were later positioned in defensive positions and I found myself in a ditch alongside a big hedge and no one in sight, as far as I could see, neither friend nor foe. The quiet stillness lasted for two hours and then someone came and cancelled the exercise. However, we were told to keep our boots on, and be ready to spring to, but I promptly took my boots off and so did the chap next to me, and we lay down and pulled our gas capes over us. It started to rain and I listened to the pitter-patter on the cape and soon fell asleep.

Reveille sounded at six a.m. and up we got to have some nice fried bacon at the field kitchen. My friend and I listened to the chaps grumbling about having no sleep. It was then we learned that we had been attacked during the night but the two of us had slept merrily on.

We were soon cleared up and in marching order but our clothes being somewhat wet, the march back was tiring. I remember our officer saying that we should be 'lively enough when we got back to barracks' and soon be dashing off to Worcester. His remarks applied to me perfectly, because I had a forty-eight-hour pass and would be on my way to meet Eva and Jeff at Cliffe.

After our last rest the depot band came out to meet us and with their lively tunes we felt very refreshed. It is quite extraordinary what martial music can do for tired soldiers.

Jimmy Brown and I continued with the others on our course, with the occasional light diversion. One day we were on 'Fire Picket', which meant being on call in case of fire or air raid. We were instructed on the handling of a fire pump, which could be attached to a motor vehicle or propelled manually. It is no easy job to run with a rolled fire hose, and to unwind it without stumbling or dropping it. The fire picket was told to remain fully clothed and lie on our beds at night, as we might be called out. I was well asleep when the air raid siren woke me and our fire call sounded. We manhandled our pump and waited. There was quite a bit of gunfire but no bombs were dropped near to us, and so no fires had to be dealt with.

One weekend Jimmy suggested exploring the countryside. It was there he told me that as a boy he had lived in Surrey. He was very interested in finding the house of David Lloyd George, the Premier during the last two years of the 1914–18 war. I have forgotten now the name of the house. We went by bus for some distance and then walked quite a long way. It was a lovely day in October, I remember. After studying a map we had obtained, Jimmy said we were getting close to our objective. I asked him why he was so interested in this particular house and he informed me that this was where his father had worked some twenty-five or thirty years before. Jimmy said he could remember the house and that the country was beginning to look familiar to him. He told me that there was a summerhouse in the woods adjoining the garden and that he had painted on a piece of wood the name he gave it and nailed it up. He did not tell me the name, so I asked him. I did not doubt that I was being told the perfect truth because Jimmy was the soul of honour.

We found the house after much searching and entered the grounds, making sure we were shielded from the house by trees and bushes. I reminded Jimmy that we were trespassing, and likely to be prosecuted if caught, but he pressed on regardless. After further progress through the wood we saw the summerhouse and, sure enough, there was the name he had given it: 'Little Grey Home in the West'. Jimmy gazed at it for some minutes, lost in his memories.

After we got back on to the road we saw a big horse chestnut tree. Quite a few nuts had fallen and Jimmy, with a mischievous grin, picked a number of them up, saying 'We shall have a laugh tonight'. We had a cup of tea somewhere and made our way back from what had been a thoroughly enjoyable outing. On arriving at barracks I saw that the barrack room was in the usual state of Sunday disarray. It is the one day in the week when no inspections take place and the troops can enjoy the glorious abandon of untidiness.

We were sleeping in double bunk-beds, wooden, one on top of the other. The chap occupying the bed above Jimmy was a very humorous cockney. Before getting into bed, and while the Cockney was not around, Jimmy put the horse chestnuts he had gathered into the bed above him. We lay expectantly in our blankets after 'lights out' had sounded. Then we heard Cockney coming, and he started cracking jokes as he got undressed, some of them directed at Jimmy who was always referred to as Jock. We didn't have much longer to wait. He pushed his feet down the blankets and let out a most unholy shriek and swore by all the gods to get even with Jocks in general, and one in particular. The room was a riot of laughter and Cockney's remarks were very rich.

The end of the course was near and we were wondering which day they would test us. Our instructor informed us with a nonchalant air, that his listeners did not appreciate, that our test would be held next day. It so happened that Jimmy and I were both on guard that night and so would not get any sleep, but I thought I might get an opportunity to read my notes. My guard came first and I was in the orderly room for the first two hours. One small light was on and it was as quiet as a church. I had brought my notes with me and quickly started to read. Quiet solitude concentrates the mind wonderfully, and I absorbed quite a lot during the two hours.

Next morning we arrived for the test and were suitably

spaced to avoid any cribbing and got down to our examination. It lasted about two hours and later in the day we returned to the room to hear the results. There were about twenty in the class and surprise, surprise, my name was read out first; I had topped the class.

When we first arrived at Aldershot we were told on one of the parades to fall out if we had not had a leave for a certain period. All 'leave' is entered in our army books, as are food ration coupons and suchlike. My last leave, shortly before I left Prestatyn, had not been entered in my army book: this had been omitted, and was a regular ploy among the staff. I can still remember the person who conveniently forgot – he was Sergeant Black and he was, prior to his call-up, a footman at Buckingham Palace.

I did not want to take a leave so soon after leaving Prestatyn so I stood fast, and again at the end of the course we were told to fall out if we were due for leave. The Sergeant-Major on looking at my AB64 asked why I had not applied before: was I deaf or had I no home to go to? My leave was granted and Eva and Jeffery were back at Nuneaton to welcome me home. We had our usual happy ten days and visited a few friends but, alas, those brief intervals passed and I was back on the train, Aldershot-bound.

Having finished what we came here to do we were given odd jobs, but got quite bored. We were waiting for a posting, and as is usual in any group of humans, rumours abounded and the stories put forward as being authentic would post most of us all round the world. The weeks passed by and still we heard nothing. We had quite a good Christmas: I had been in the army nearly two years and it was my second Christmas in uniform.

It was shortly after this that we heard where we were going. Some eighteen or so, including Jimmy Brown, were being sent to HQ 21 Army Group in London. We considered ourselves lucky going to such a big HQ. The 21 Army Group was formed, of course, for the invasion of Europe, it comprised the British 2nd Army, the Canadian 1st Army, Polish Divisions and Free French detachments. General Montgomery and his choice of Staff Officers had come from Italy to take command. Also a number of divisions of first-class quality came back from Italy to lead the invasion. I have read many books on these matters since the end of the war. Indeed, only very recently I read a biography of General Alexander; the denuding of troops in the Mediterranean was a much contested argument, but Alex, as he was generally known, achieved remarkable success with limited forces.

Jimmy went into Civil Affairs and I to Camp Commandment's Office.

The HQ had taken over a big school and many buildings near by. We were billeted in some so-called 'luxury flats' but all the luxury had gone when troops entered. They were completely bare; we slept on bed boards and straw palliasses and our dining-hall was in the Olympia Exhibition building. We worked quite hard from about eight a.m. to six p.m., with one day per week off.

Enemy bombing had been very intermittent for some time but it seemed to increase with my arrival in London. It may have been the German attempt to cause some disruption to the build-up for the invasion of Europe and we had quite a packet each night.

One effect of this was my friend Jimmy began to get very jumpy. We went out in the evening but as soon as the air raid warning sounded Jimmy would be on his way to the underground railway. Having reached the trains one could ride at will and tickets were not requested until one left a station. One evening we were walking near Trafalgar Square when the sirens sounded and very quickly the anti-aircraft guns were going off. We tried, with lots more people, to get to the tube at a nearby station, but found it closed, and later learned that trains passing under the Thames were stopped during a raid. It was pitch dark apart from shells bursting in the sky. Jimmy shouted, 'Come on, Bill,' so I followed, and some people got kicked in the rush. We reached the underground platform which was crowded, full of people getting bedded down for

Bill enjoying his leave, 1944

the night. This was a regular feature of London nights: people had their spot on the platform and returned to it each night. A painted line divided the sleeping area from the trains. We decided it was better to ride around on the trains in comfort than to stand on the station platform.

All went well until we emerged above ground only to see bombs exploding. We changed trains at the first stop and were soon underground again like rabbits to their burrows.

Eventually it was arranged that people living some distance from London could take their weekly day off as two together each fortnight. This suited me fine, as I would be able to get home. The only snag was we did not get a travel warrant, so we had to pay or resort to ulterior methods.

I had no compunction, in the circumstances then existing, in resorting to less than honest tactics. The trains were crowded with people in uniform and the majority would have travel warrants. The tricks we pulled were many and varied when the ticket collector came along and I did not pay once over a period of six months. One night in my compartment, which was packed with troops, a sergeant sat in the corner and when the ticket collector opened the door the sergeant pulled out a piece of paper and said 'party' and the ticket collector turned away without looking at the travel warrant, phoney or otherwise.

One always had to have a pass to travel and this was readily obtainable. We office people wrote our own pass and got it signed by a senior NCO. On one occasion I was travelling back to London and after leaving the train and walking along the platform at Euston, two 'Red Caps' (Military Police) stopped me and asked to see my pass. That day was 1 May and my pass was up on 31 April. There being only thirty days in April, any fool should have seen it was a clerical error, but no, I was marched off to the RTO's office on the station. They phoned my unit and, having learned that I was known there, they let me go saying that I would face a charge of AWOL (absent without leave). The RSM for the HQ was a Scots Guardsman and two days later I was marched into the Camp Commandant's office to be questioned by Captain Brown, the adjutant. When I explained the position he laughed and said 'case dismissed'.

We tried to visit places of interest on our free days and one of these visits took us to Lord's cricket ground. I cannot remember who the competing teams were, but I do recall that I saw that great batsman Wally Hammond knocking the bowling about.

General Montgomery spent more time away from the HQ than in it. He inspected all units who were to take part in 'Overlord' which was the code for the invasion of Europe. The divisions were spread all over the country, but I believe everybody involved had seen Monty before the balloon went up.

There were many conferences at the school and we saw many VIPs pass our office including General Eisenhower, Lord Tedder, Winston Churchill, Anthony Eden and many more. We seldom saw Monty, but on one occasion when I had been duty clerk, I was proceeding from the Camp Commandant's Office to the main school and as I passed the gateway, which was the main entrance to the grounds from the road, Monty entered: he was about twenty yards behind me so when I reached the school entrance I stopped at the foot of the steps, turned towards him, came to attention and threw a salute. He saluted back and said 'good morning'. The next time I was to hear his voice was in Brussels.

The nightly raids continued and some men of the HQ were killed. It so happened I was duty clerk two nights later. I answered a phone call from Euston railway station; they were expecting a body to go north on a certain train – relatives claiming a private funeral. I knew nothing about this, so I called the duty officer, Major Pavey; another raid was in progress and bombs were dropping fairly near. The officer suggested that I go to the shelter and no second invitation was necessary.

The whole country was expecting a landing in France almost any day, and we at HQ knew these expectations would soon be fulfilled. The date of 'Overlord' was known to very few, but the place of invasion was known to many more. I knew a few months before but security was very tight and the enemy were taken by surprise, as post-war literature demonstrates. It has always appeared most remarkable to me that people in the UK remained 'mum' when so much was happening. The advertising campaign helped, I am certain. Posters were stuck up everywhere, stating 'Walls have ears', 'Keep mum – she's worth it' and many more. Some weeks prior to the invasion of France all leave was stopped. Corporal Clay in our office, who came from Hinckley in Leicestershire, apparently had a wife who disbelieved her husband concerning leave and came up to London to find out. The flying bombs had started, and had been christened doodle-bugs. Corporal Clay met his wife and took her into a restaurant, but as soon as they started to eat, a doodle-bug landed outside. They finished up under the table. She became convinced of the leave position and with some haste made her way back to Leicestershire.

The night the flying bombs started I had stayed in the flats. When the men came in they were very enthusiastic about the number of 'enemy planes' being shot down. This first night of the doodle-bug menace, my cousin Len's house was demolished. They lived at Croydon Road, Beddington. Len, who was in the RAF, was at home on leave, and by some miracle Grace, Len and Audrey crawled out of the wreckage. I will have more to say of this later.

The enemy night raids and the flying bombs caused us much annoyance but did not help the enemy in any way. Nothing happened at our HQ to indicate when the invasion would take place but the HQ was split up and a good number of people were moved out to complete what was known as forward HQ and we who remained were known as rear HQ. Within a few weeks of this happening we began to pack our things, office equipment etc, as we were moving out of London. Our move was to Virginia Water in Surrey and there we were accommodated in tents.

It was quite a relief to get away from the bombing. We were actually living alongside a golf course. Jimmy and I had a few rounds but our stay was not long enough to improve our game.

That memorable day dawned, 6 June, 1944, known then, and subsequently, as 'D' Day'. The Allies had landed in Normandy. The enemy did not believe this to be the main landing and so did not commit the forces they ought to have done. This misreading of our intentions was fostered by propaganda and by Churchill's public radio broadcasts. He led them to believe that we should attack in more than one place, and so we got a good lodgement without too much opposition. I have never ceased to have the greatest admiration for the men who made the initial assault.

Before this invasion of France took place and before we had left London, everyone was given seven days' embarkation leave and another brief interval of happiness followed.

Eva, Jeff and I paid a visit to Lichfield to see my parents; we went by train from Nuneaton to Lichfield, Trent Valley. Mother, Father, George and Bertha met us at the station and we then had to walk two miles via country lanes.

Jeffery was much admired and was carried some of the way, first by Uncle George and then Grandad. I can recall that walk very distinctly. Father tried not to ask too many questions but I realised he wanted to know so much and he guessed that I could answer some of his questions. We had a very pleasant time and Mother obtained food of adequate proportions despite the rationing. We walked around Lichfield, I recall, looking for old friends, but I don't think we found any.

The leave came to an end and Eva and I wondered how long it would be before our next meeting. Future leave would depend on the success of the military effort in France. Back at camp we were all interested in our next move. It was not long in coming; we started to pack up again.

Chapter Eleven

All the British ports in the south were being used and I tried to get to know where we should embark but no one seemed to know. An advance party from rear HQ left some days before the rest of us. We heard, but it was never confirmed, that they had gone via London docks and were hit in the Channel.

When our turn came to leave for France reveille sounded at two a.m. and we were soon aboard our trucks. Quite a long tree-lined avenue led up to the main road, and my hope was that we should make for a western embarkation port, so when we reached the main road and turned left, I was quite happy. The convoy was very long, there seemed to be trucks as far as one could see. To sit in the back of a truck, I believe ours was a six ton, becomes quite peculiar after a time. The trees and other objects rush away from you, as opposed to sitting in the front of a vehicle when objects race towards you.

I did not recognise the road or places we passed through. After a couple of hours or so we pulled off the road into a wooded area and were told we were stopping for breakfast. The resident cooks had been busy and dished up a meal of bacon and sausage. I can still recall how good it tasted. It was still dark, the trees not helping in this respect. We were told to hurry and were soon on the trucks again.

The dawn was soon breaking and I thought how lovely the countryside looked. We began to enter a built-up area but it was some time before I knew where we were; we actually were entering Gosport and that was our port of embarkation. It was most noticeable how much the road was cut up with the heavy traffic, including the pavements. The movement of troops and equipment had been in progress to France for some seven or eight weeks and my guess would be that some twenty divisions or more were now in France with their thousands of vehicles.

It is still astonishing to me that the enemy did not bomb our ports of embarkation and all the traffic pouring into them. Undoubtedly we had to thank the RAF for this; we had complete mastery of the air.

We finally halted near to the quay and I was soon looking around. The nearest ship to us was a LST (a type of Tank Landing Craft) from which German prisoners were coming ashore. They marched past us and I recall how scruffy they appeared. They looked listless, tired and, it seemed at the time, evil; I believe they had been through a terrible time. It took quite a while to clear this human cargo.

We started going aboard with a minimum of delay and it was a relief to stretch our legs and look around. We had minor problems getting aboard, the vehicles had to be backed on and some drivers weren't too capable. These LST's were designed, as the name implies, to put tanks ashore. The end of the vessel was one big door, let down like a drawbridge, and when it was down, depending on how close the vessel could get in to land, it often left an expanse of water, some few feet in our case and not very deep. Vehicles were raised on a lift to get on top deck and then they were chained and bolted through each wheel.

We lay around all day smoking and sleeping. In the evening we began to move but not very far, we dropped anchor close to the Isle of Wight, opposite the Needles. These were the occasions when the card schools came into prominence, but we had no card sharps in our immediate circle.

When it began to get dark we moved off and an air raid warning sounded about the same time. I don't recall any boat drill; perhaps the authorities felt pretty confident.

I have always been prone to seasickness and have found the best plan is to lie down. With this in mind I climbed into our truck and tried to go to sleep. Despite the momentous occasion and strange happenings, I was singularly successful. Sleep must have come to me very readily because when I woke up after a very good night's rest, the sun was up and shining brilliantly. Men were squatting all over the deck eating porridge. I was soon on my way to the galley to receive porridge and bacon. It was a beautiful morning and as we gazed at the French coast it appeared to be very peaceful.

The thing that was so eye-catching was the amount of shipping in the Channel. It appeared to me to be very compact and I immediately thought what a target for enemy bombers, but nothing happened by way of attack.

We appeared to be sailing along the coast, about a mile out, in the direction of Cherbourg, but well away from that area. The address system on the ship opened up and we were addressed by the Captain. He gave us a running commentary of our position and approach. It seemed just then to be more like a holiday cruise than warfare; we appeared to glide along with no purpose.

Eventually we came to Mulberry Harbour. This harbour has gained much acclaim and rightly so; it was made and towed across the Channel at its widest part, possibly one hundred miles. It was essentially a gigantic concrete block, fitted together to make a calm anchorage.

We docked and the lorries began to move. Those on the top deck drove straight off the deck on to built-up trellis work, and away we went down on to the beach. Large-mesh steel was laid over the sand to prevent traffic getting bogged down. We travelled over the sand and on to grassland and the first thing I noticed were crowds of POW behind wire, waiting to be evacuated. It was a very hot day and also dusty; we continued moving through country lanes – the road surface being much lower than the hedges and banks. It is known as *bocage* country – poor terrain for tanks but good infantry country.

We pulled into a field and the first person to speak to me was Jimmy Brown: 'Och man, but you've aged a wee bit.' When I looked at the other chaps I gathered what he meant. The grey dust had covered us and our hair and eyebrows appeared quite white. There were water taps in this field, the engineers having been busy, but notices were prominent telling us not to drink the water. Everyone was tired, hot and thirsty but I resisted the temptation to drink the water. Late in the afternoon we had tea, white bread and butter and tinned peaches.

The engineers had built some water troughs for washing and I was so engaged when a number of troops from the Hertfordshire Regiment were close by. I could see they were in the 11th Armoured Division, so I started chatting to them. I asked them if they knew Jack Berks, my cousin, who was I knew in their regiment. They were very interested and keen to know how he was progressing. I had been told before I left England that Jack had been wounded within hours of landing in France. Whether he was lucky or otherwise I don't know, but he is alive today with just one leg slightly shorter than the other: Jack had been in a group armed with Sten guns, and having been told to pile arms they did so, but one gun fell over and a shot went through Jack's leg.

We got ourselves organised and had a big tent under trees as our office, and an adjoining field was where we slept in a cider apple orchard. That night Jerry came over and bombed us; we suffered no casualties, but the information tent went up in flames.

Someone told us, as we were lying under the trees one night, that an American vessel had been wrecked on the beach with plenty of goodies on board. Several chaps went even though it was a long walk, but not me. I thought it much too hazardous with the doubtful clearance of mines. They came back eventually and we had a good feed. One of the group even gave me a large tin of peaches and I promptly put it into my kit-bag and carried it around for nearly eighteen months until I had my first leave and took it home for Eva and Jeff.

We stayed at this spot for several weeks. The battle of Falaise had taken place and the German 15th Army was annihilated. The whole Allied front surged forward and we then prepared to move. Driver and truck were allocated to our section but the driver was a misfit. Staff/Sergeant-Major York told him to get aboard and see how he performed but he soon drove into a gatepost and got the sack. S/Sgt-Major. York asked me to drive but I declined as I had never driven anything bigger than a small car. He then got Ralph Lee to drive as he had had army experience of trucks, and all went well.

This journey was quite momentous, as I will relate. Before I leave Normandy I would like to describe a day Jimmy and I had in Bayeux. We were camped only a mile or two from this small town which has a famous cathedral. We walked into Bayeux and saw troops laying out a new cemetery outside the town. My wife and I spent a motoring holiday in Normandy some twenty-five years later and the cemetery was a most beautiful spot. The sight Jimmy and I saw was mud and chaos. Since the town was very poor we could not even buy ourselves a drink. We went into the cathedral to see the famous tapestry. I am sure Jimmy and I were not sorry to be moving on to pastures new.

Before I had left my wife I told her how I would let her know where I was. I would, in my letters, wish to be remembered to fictitious people; the first letter of each Christian name would spell the nearest town to me. Eva got the message and soon had a map out. In this way she kept track of my movements and never told anyone.

Chapter Twelve

We began our movement from Normandy in a long convoy. The roads were in very poor condition with frequent shell holes, and at times we had to leave the road and travel on the adjoining fields. Apart from obvious signs of battle, the first thing I noticed was a terrifically large ammunition dump. I saw many such later, but none quite so large, with explosives of every conceivable type and size.

We soon entered the area of Caen, and the destruction was appalling. In my mind I compared it to Coventry but I soon realised how lightly Coventry had escaped in comparison. Caen had seen so much fighting and had to be reduced by heavy bombers before it was taken. The road we took was over the rubble and at one point we were as high as a church roof we passed. It was here we lost our convoy and from then on the blind were leading the blind. We lost ourselves completely in one small town; I was more interested in the town than finding our way through it. Having parted company with our convoy we had lost our food supply and arrangements or information as to finding any nourishment. We travelled many hours and eventually came to the river Seine at a small place which I believe was named Vernon. All bridges over rivers, canals etc, had been destroyed and the advancing Allies had replaced them with Bailey bridges. These were of flat metal and very effective, being extensively used throughout the war.

Some time after the war, when visiting my Uncle Fred, my father's youngest brother who retired with the rank of Lt Colonel in the Royal Engineers, he told me he was with Captain Bailey when they invented the now famous Bailey Bridge which was named after that captain during the war. We crossed the Seine and proceeded north. It was only a mile or so after this that the truck we were travelling in decided to refuse to go any further. The countryside at this point was very pleasant and wooded but we were hungry and not very happy. Many vehicles and troops were going our way and from someone we obtained water, tea and a big pot. Our sacked young driver was told to dig a small hole at the side of the road and light a fire in it. We put an iron bar across and waited for a cuppa. This nitwit of a chap upset the pot, put the fire out and we lost our water. Being nearest to him I told him in army language what a delight he was.

The mine detector men had removed and tested for three feet or so all along the roads and pegged white tape down. Notices were also along the road warning against stepping beyond the tape. S/Sgt-Major York said he would have to attend to the calls of nature and I felt the same. York gave a good jump towards the wood and I followed him. Some distance into the wood we found a building and inside, a Frenchman. We were able to wash and to test our minimal French with the Frenchman who appeared to be in charge of an electrical sub-station.

Back on the road we received help from a breakdown lorry and after some time had passed they got us going.

Yorky decided that we should pull into a farmyard for the night, which we did. It was a typical French farm. We each had thoughts of something to eat and drink but were sadly disappointed. The farmer let us leave the truck in the farmyard, but that was about where his hospitality ended. I remember we did go into the house and he gave us a tiny drop of liqueur. They had no room in the house for us, which was a very bare, cold place, and so we looked round the farm. The farmer told us that if we heard anyone about in the night it would be German soldiers coming out of the woods looking for food. My first choice of a bed was on top of a flat, straw rick, but one colleague suggested Jerry might put a match to it. After some discussion three of us stayed on the truck and the other three went elsewhere.

I occupied the rear or open end of the vehicle with my rifle handy. I suppose we had been dozing for some two hours or so when I heard movements. More footsteps, or what appeared to be footsteps, were heard on the cobbled farmyard and then a voice.

With some stealth I grabbed my rifle and tried to look into the yard. Then a voice, which sounded somewhat exasperated, assailed the night air. The voice was unrecognisable to me, so I got up, and with the help of a torch, saw the farmer trying to get a horse back into the stable. The following morning we had to wash and shave under the yard pump.

The misfit driver had spent the night in a small farm building and came out saying someone was in the shed he had occupied. Yorky asked me to look in, so, taking my torch, I found a young donkey inside with which this young chap had spent the night. I told the S/Sgt-Major and he told the young chap 'that made two of them'. We had some breakfast, but from whence it came I have no idea.

We pushed on and then the countryside gradually became less devastated. In the afternoon we stopped and Yorky insisted that we smarten ourselves up a little. Having done this we proceeded to enter Brussels. The Belgian capital had suffered very little damage and in time we entered the Guards' barracks. Barracks are never pleasant places but this place was awful: dark, cold and depressing. Electric light in Brussels was off most of the time and no food had caught up with us. The problem as I understood it was that the Channel ports had not been opened up and so all supplies had to come from Normandy.

The position was causing some concern – I had a friend in the supply division and he told me that the ammunition supply was for three days only. The food we were consuming during the first few days I was in Brussels was captured enemy rations and it was, in some cases, inedible. We had no bread, so had to try and eat German biscuits and jam; the former must have contained cement. I saw a man soak a biscuit in hot tea and then jump on it and it still remained whole. Fortunately, these privations only lasted for a few days.

A shop where we obtained some food opened up and called itself Café Blightly. I recall we could buy delicious biscuits as big as a saucer and think it was in a street known as Jardin Botanique.

My stay in Brussels lasted for some months and I got to know it quite well. Promotion was offered to me but I declined it. My company, the Prudential, were making my army pay up to the salary I was getting at my call-up and any increase in the former would be deducted from the latter.

Material things soon improved, even to the extent of having decent toilets fitted. The most notable event was the opening of the Montgomery Club. Almost next door to the barracks was a magnificent residence which I learned was formerly the home of a distinguished Belgian family. This magnificent place was fitted out as a club for service people. For Jimmy and me it became our home with billiard rooms, table tennis, café, and reading rooms with comfortable easy chairs. We were there every night.

The English daily papers were there each day and Jimmy could hardly get me away from them. We were often in conversation with troops from forward areas. One night I bumped into Bill Widdop; we were equally surprised. We were last together in Market Rasen nearly three years before and had much to talk about. Jimmy and I were playing billiards one evening and he was reflecting on his next shot when I saw some Top Brass come into the room. General Montgomery came up to speak to me. I stood to attention but my friend, oblivious of the august presence, was damning the shot that I had left him. On looking up he came to and nearly stamped his billiard cue through the boards when coming to attention.

The enemy at this time trained flying bombs on to Brussels and one dropped quite close to the barracks. It must have been before the Monty Club opened because all the chaps were out girl-hunting, an interest I never acquired. I was alone reading.

Christmas 1944 was a wonderful affair for troops stationed in the Belgian capital. A large store was taken over for Christmas Day, I believe it was the 'Bon Marché' and we all had a sumptuous meal and plenty to drink.

My friend and I were very interested in things and places of historical note, and one day we decided to visit the site of the Battle of Waterloo; trams went the whole way. Having read much about the battle I was more than interested.

The scene of battle is laid out under cover and an English-speaking guide gave us a running commentary, which we thoroughly enjoyed.

The Belgians could not do enough for the British and Allied troops and the first ones to enter Brussels were overwhelmed with kindness. During my first week or so in the town I went a walk round with the chap that had driven our truck, Ralph Lee. We stopped, looking into a shop window, when a lady of doubtful age and appearance threw her arms round Ralph and kissed him, crying 'Mon ami, mon ami'. I sidled round the corner and managed to escape such attention.

Jimmy and I went to a local church which opened a refreshment room where we obtained tea and buns. We made friends with a Belgian lady who was one of the helpers. Jimmy could converse with her – his French was quite good. She asked us one day if we would like to go and have lunch with her family on Sunday, so we accepted. Knowing she had a small daughter, we took our chocolate ration. When we gave it to the girl after the meal she said it was dirty brown stuff, and the mother told us it was the first chocolate she had seen, hence her doubtful acceptance of it.

We had a very good meal and I can still recall having three helpings of soup and roast beef. This greatly surprised us because no meat was available in Brussels. The husband told us in broken English that he had some good friends in the country.

Some time after landing in France, in one of my wife's letters, she told me that John Coltman had been home on embarkation leave and was now on his way to India and in a subsequent letter I learned that Gwen was expecting a child. John and Gwen had obtained a house in Nuneaton soon after we moved there and it was of some comfort to both John and me to know they could visit each other.

John has always kept a diary and when with them recently he read from a 1945 diary in which he had recorded the birth a son. Looking back to these years my wife and I have remarked how providential this birth was.

Anthony is now a solicitor with two daughters. His only sister, Marie, some fourteen years older, died when she was thirty-eight years old and John and Gwen's life revolves around their son and his family.

The enemy had been on the defensive or retreat since the allies landed, but at Christmas they mounted an attack of considerable size and scope and drove a wedge of some miles. Orders were issued to us at rear HQ so wherever we went we had to have our rifle and ammunition with us. This quite alarmed the local Belgians; one lady ran after me in the street and said 'You won't leave us will you?'

After a week or so the weather improved and the RAF joined in and stopped the enemy, and the troops cleared up. Reading of this event subsequently it appears to have been Hitler's final gamble.

The American daylight air raids carried out on Germany at this time were quite tremendous. When we had been at Waterloo we climbed what seemed hundreds of steps up the mound, and being tired, sat down and gazed aloft. The sky was filled with planes as far as one could see, large bombers mostly 'Flying Fortresses' – we knew the end of the war could not be far away.

In the early spring of 1945 I was moved from HQ 21st Army Group, together with a number of others, to Netherlands District HQ at Tilburg in Holland. We went by train from the Gare du Nord, where I was surprised to see a number of British rail coaches.

On arriving at our destination an NCO told us that a clerk was wanted in G Ops, and another by the Assistant Chaplain General. I told him the Chaplain would suit me and off to my new job I went.

We were billeted in some barracks and the Chaplain had an office in a damaged private house. The Padre was a pleasant man who had a car and driver, and I plus two old Dutchmen completed his staff. It was soon apparent to me that we could all be dispensed with without loss to the Allied war effort.

About three letters a day was my maximum typing effort. Often some of these would be personal letters to the Archbishop of Canterbury.

The Padre got upset one day when I typed a letter in which he quoted from the book of Ecclesiastes and I typed another, though similar, name. He asked how often I read the Bible and I very nearly told him where to get off. He often took me out with him in the car, and the driver and I were given chocolate. Mostly on these journeys we went as far forward as we were allowed and the Chaplain called on local priests. One day we were turned back very hurriedly by British troops who told us we were nearly up to the enemy. On another occasion we travelled from Holland into Germany and on our return we were stopped at the border and told by an Intelligence Corps chap that no one could enter Holland from Germany. The Padre nearly blew his top but after some consultation in a nearby office we were permitted to return.

The condition of the local population was much worse in Holland than in France or Belgium. People would gather round the exit to our dining-hall clamouring for scraps. Standing at the rear of the group one day I noticed a tall, white-haired, gaunt old man whom I immediately felt urged to help. Notices were displayed forbidding the handing out of food, but despite this I obtained an extra helping of rice pudding and took most of it to the old boy. He scraped it out of my dixie with his fingers like a famished wolf.

About this time a temporary truce was arranged to enable the Allies to drop food to the Dutch. The Padre took this opportunity to go up to Rotterdam and I accompanied him. He went into a large building and I stayed on the outside and immediately German soldiers pestered me for cigarettes. They kept up *Englisch zigaretten* and I replied *nicht zigaretten*, and didn't part with any. What the Padre did and who he saw I cannot remember, even if I ever knew. He was often very reticent, but quite forthright in his letters. He wrote a letter requesting the recall of a front-line Padre, stating that he lacked the nous to do a front-line job.

We did not stay too long at Tilburg, but the war ended while we were there. The friend I came up with from Brussels had gone to work in G Ops. In his job he handled situation reports and he told me before the news broke that hostilities would cease at 24.00 hours. The Padre held an open-air service and that was the only time I saw or heard him officiate.

It seemed to me quite remarkable how quickly war material, tanks and field guns etc. came pouring back, the day following cessation of fighting.

The great news we all wanted to hear was later published, stating the order for demobilisation. The information was posted up and a big crowd gathered to read it. I made a note of the salient points and worked out my discharge number would be twenty-nine. The method involved was quite ingenious and fair, based on age at entry into the forces, years served and several other factors, but some chaps could not work out their own number. We soon realised that knowing one's demob number was a long way from knowing when we should get discharged but we we did learn that more men were in groups twenty-four, twenty-five and twenty-six than any other.

We moved from Tilburg to The Hague and occupied some nice offices on the seaward side of the town, actually close to Scheveningen. This place, I would think, had been a very pleasant seaside resort in pre-war days but now it was fenced off with barbed wire.

The Padre was demob number one and was soon on his way. For me this was a most peculiar period. I sat in the office all day with nothing to do and no one came. I read whatever I could. A number of us went into the town each evening and drank very watery beer. I noticed my left index finger started to swell and after a couple of days was an enormous size, so a visit to the MO seemed indicated.

He looked at it and said 'I'll cut that out.' A big sergeant held me down and the doctor made the necessary cuts and a black nurse poured penicillin on my hand, promptly dropping the bottle. They put my arm in a sling and thus I walked around for days.

Once the war was over it was quite interesting to see how the Dutch people dealt with the people who had co-operated with the Germans. They were rounded up and segregated and each morning we saw groups of them being marched off, but their ultimate fate I never discovered. The different languages on the continent were all a trial to me but none more so that the Dutch and Flemish. Between Scheveningen and The Hague was the principal site where the Germans launched the V2, the rocket bomb. These V2s were fired several miles into the air and dropped on London without any warning, but fortunately the period of attack was not too long because of the Allied advance. I walked past the site many times and was interested in seeing what I could. The district was good class residential, the surrounding houses were badly damaged but whether this was caused by our attacks or misfiring of rockets I never discovered.

My enigmatic existence continued with no interruptions and then one morning a young Padre walked into the office, searched the cupboard, found four bottles of communion wine (which I had inspected many times with conflicting emotions) and walked off with them.

It was June now and the weather quite good. The Dutch Government had been in London for most of the war I understand and had now returned. Our HQ had been responsible for civil administration as well as military and so its work was gradually terminated, and we received our marching orders. I was soon on the train with others and our destination was Bruges, or Brugge, as the Flemish say.

There was an air of nonchalance about the troops, I noticed now. We travelled on a train with broken windows and one chap opened the carriage door while going along, and it swung backwards and forwards. I thought there would be a bang and flying glass if it hit a bridge or another train. But no, we travelled without mishap across that flat, uninteresting land. On arrival at Bruges we were met and marched to an area of wasteland near or in the town where tents were pitched. This was a holding unit and we just had to wait on the decision of the powers that be. The military standard that was kept up was quite good. We were enclosed in a wire compound and could only leave the area on official business.

It was funny the jobs men were given, to keep them busy, with the Belgians looking through the wire at us. The remarks floating about such as skits on Winston Churchill's famous 1940 speech, 'Never in the history of human misery have so many been . . . about by so few', were rife. There were several hundred of us and about six to a tent. We were a mixed bag in our tent, an old soldier more artful than the proverbial dodger, a divinity student whom I chatted with, a likeable man named George who had a small fur business in London, but the others I have forgotten. The old soldier asked us one morning if we wanted to get out into the town and we all said yes. He then told us to do as he said and to follow him.

Each morning there was a muster parade and after a casual inspection, various sections fell out or were marched off by different NCOs. Our old soldier stepped out in front and in a loud voice shouted 'Dental party 'shun, dental party left turn, quick march' – and the six of us marched into town. We went into a café, had a drink and a good laugh and someone suggested a trip to Blankenberge. Trams ran all the way to the coast and travel was free to people in uniform, and we enjoyed the short trip. When we got to Blankenberge we found it had received some damage and were amused to see dummy guns on the promenade.

We wandered about the shops and then saw a notice for 'Egg and Chips, English Style' and placed our order. Food was still very short so this was quite a surprise. Having seen the place we lay in the sun and whiled the afternoon away. One chap said 'I wonder if they have missed us yet', but we weren't worried. Eventually we got a tram and wended our way back. On entering the camp one had to give one's name and number at the entrance gate to military police. I was first and the Redcap said 'Where have you been?' and I replied 'Just wandering about' and then he told me I was on guard, and parade was in half an hour. George was the only other one of us. They all helped George and me to get ready; our webbing equipment had not been worn for two years or so nor rifle cleaned. Perspiring freely, we just made it. George informed me that he had never done a guard so I gave him some hurried instruction, telling him to get in the centre rank behind me. All went off without mishap. We paraded in the yard of a school occupied by nuns and later I was posted to do sentry duty at the entrance to our camp. A small river or perhaps a canal ran along the opposite side of the lane and the croaking of frogs in the otherwise quiet night was all that disturbed me.

Bruges is a lovely old town and I would say mediaeval in appearance. Some military parade was to be held and some mayor was to inspect the troops. The troops were from one of the crack divisions, I believe it was the 49th Infantry, and a very fine turnout they gave. Our unit CO told us to keep in the background and make our way into the town in twos and threes.

I was in this town for quite a few weeks. One Sunday, as the locals, dressed in black, were wending their way to church, a number of us were paraded and marched to a military documentation centre. The result was our army books were stamped 'available for SEAC' – South-East Asia Command. I was quite concerned and so were many others. Everyone wanted to get home, not go out East. I was most perturbed how I should break the news to my wife, who had had a bad time with Jeff's health. That evening I went into the NAAFI to write to her, but after much thought tore the letter up and wrote later, but did not mention going East – which as events turn out, was wise.

Chapter Thirteen

We were lying in our tent one evening when the news broke that an atom bomb had been dropped on Japan and we were left wondering what would happen next. Thinking how best I could influence my own posting I wrote to my old friend Jimmy Brown asking if he might do anything. It was a day or two later, we were just finishing our midday meal, when the loudspeaker requested me to attend the orderly room at once. A number of people immediately piped up 'Far East here we come', but I thought it could be something less unpleasant. The orderly room staff informed me that I was being posted to Bad Oeynhausen in Germany that evening. They gave me various papers and told me to get packed up and catch a certain train.

I knew that this was Jimmy Brown's work, but how he had managed it I couldn't guess. Later he told me in response to my letter that he had spoken to his OC telling him where I was, awaiting a posting, and that we were old friends and just to add weight that I was one of the best clerks in the army!

The journey into Germany was very tedious. The carriages were badly damaged and we were crowded in. We drew from a pack of cards to obtain a position for the night. The places competed for were the luggage racks, the floor and half a seat: we spent a disturbed night as the train crawled along. We arrived at our destination in the middle of the night and I rather think it was the second night. The authorities had decreed that non-fraternisation would apply between Allied troops and Germans and some soldiers were soon on a charge for going into German houses.

It was very quiet when I walked out of the station; a military policeman told me where to go and I spent the rest of the night on a couch in a large room. Jimmy came round for me and took me for breakfast. Jimmy had always been in 'Civil Affairs' at 21st Army Group but now it was altered. We now belonged to Allied Control Commission, Germany. I was put to work in 'Public Safety' – we were the Admin. HQ of Police and Fire Services. It really was starting from scratch, and I dealt with correspondence relating to design of uniforms.

In recording all this, that I am now writing, I find most of it easy to recall, but there are periods that appear quite blank and my posting into Germany appears to be one. I did not stay long in Bad Oeynhausen as our section of Public Safety was moved to Bünde.

I was very happy with the men I was working with, they were some of the best I met in the army. One was Vince Forte, an Italian. He told me that he came to England with his parents when he was eight years old and could not speak a word of English. They prospered and today are very successful. Vince was often asking me to visit him after the war; indeed, I have done so, and my wife found him and his wife most interesting. Vince's uncle is the now well-known Chairman of Trust House Forte's Hotel group and incidentally a millionaire. We write at Christmas but I never kept in touch with anyone else, other than Jimmy.

At Bünde we occupied German houses affording minimum comfort. There was a cigar factory in this small town, and for reasons I have now quite forgotten, I called there one day and was given two boxes of cigars, one of which I brought home for my father.

When in London I mentioned how the bombing upset my friend but he recovered his nerve completely later. While in Bünde an incident occurred which proves this. The house we were in accomodated about eight of us clerks, and a couple of runners, the army term for messengers. One of the latter was frequently getting drunk and he came in one night fighting drunk. He stood in the door of the sitting room holding a knife and shouted 'where is he?' He then picked up a chair and hurled it at the centre light and we were in darkness. A number of us got our cigarette lighters out but Jimmy had his alight first and calmly walked up to the inebriated fool and took the knife from him.

Life in Bünde was pleasant, if monotonous. For a time I was clerk to a man I have often read of since the war – he was Chief Constable of Somerset for a time. The military personnel of the Control Commission were gradually being replaced by people recruited in England, both male and female. They wore khaki uniform but no regimental badge, or badge of rank. We had a number of policemen come to see us and also some staff from the Home Office. But it seemed to me that the soldiers always acted as duty clerk, and this came round about every ten days or so – and of course we only got a fraction of the money the civilians were getting. The duty clerk would receive each night by phone a situation report from each of five different areas within the British Zone. I was duty clerk one night when I received a report that a goods train had been attacked and pilfered. I rang the duty officer but could only get his batman, and the former said it could wait till morning. When he came round in the morning I told him some home truths and was really rude to him. He could have put me on a charge but he didn't – we were alone, so he would have had no witnesses.

Everything seems to take second place to rank in the army as was shown another night when I was duty clerk. The phone rang and I answered to hear it was the War Office in London. Some well-spoken chap asked a number of questions which I was able to answer and he became very chatty, and then he suddenly asked me to whom he was speaking. On hearing my rank his tone became very chilly and he rang off.

About this time the authorities supplied a number of cycles to our HQ for the pleasure of the staff. I went with a number of others, cycling round the German countryside and it was quite an experience. We stopped at a half-timbered country inn. There would be about twenty or so of us including one or two ATS girls. There were fruit trees growing along the roadside, and I have noted this feature a few times since then on our holiday tours of Germany. I understand that the first fruit trees planted on German roadsides were part of the reparations from the Franco-German War of 1870.

On another occasion we went a good distance and then walked for a while through a forest. This is remembered because in the forest we came across a piece of metal foil which had been dropped by our bombers to confuse the German defences- it would have shown up on their radar and the planes could divert elsewhere.

Looking back now to the time I spent in *Deutschland* after hostilities ceased, I realise I did not avail myself of all the sightseeing opportunities. One Sunday I recall an outing to Hamelin (Hameln), the 'Pied Piper's' town, but I preferred to stay and read the English Sunday papers.

Another move to keep the troops happy was made when short leaves were granted to us in Germany to spend forty-eight hours in Brussels. Vince Forte and I arranged to go together and we had quite a good time.

Vince at this time was unmarried and he had a girlfriend in Brussels, presumably he had met her when he was stationed there. We had plenty of money to spend and I bought a number of presents for Eva and Jeff. Meccano sets were available in Brussels and Jeff was later very pleased with them. For Eva I bought silk-like underwear and nylon stockings which, if obtainable in England, were on coupons. I also remember buying some shoes for Eva, the open-toe style which was the latest fashion. We had a few laughs buying the right sizes. Fortunately I had obtained from Eva her sizes, but to relate these to Belgian sizes was quite difficult. The Belgian girls in the shops giggled and first my wife to them was very small and then very large. But in the event they all fitted and my good lady was delighted.

The Black Market was very rife on the continent, but I personally thought it wrong and had very little to do with it, but I did sell the odd packet of cigarettes in Holland. Some men were very active and very keen to make money, but on demobilisation were caught with more money than they could exchange and a lot of them lost quite large amounts. Even so the British Exchequer still suffered and I remember reading in the press some two or more years after the war ended that the Treasury had lost a million or two. Cigarettes were the main currency in wartime – they would buy anything.

For most people who saw the human misery in Germany immediately after hostilities ceased, it was a scene never to be forgotten. Train-loads of derelict people were conveyed in cattle trucks, they were mostly displaced persons being sorted out by the Allies. Hitler had throughout the war moved people forcibly to do his bidding, and great numbers ended up in concentration camps. When the Allies overran these places they filmed life in the camps. Never since the Dark Ages, I believe, had humans been subject to such ignominy and torture. The Allies had then, quite rightly in my opinion, compelled the German people to see these films.

The people I saw were being returned to their homeland in many cases, but many had lost all contact with their former life and had to be accommodated in displaced persons' camps. They appeared to be crammed into the cattle trucks, supporting their fellow inmates, looking over the top, in that special thraldom of hope that distils slowly to the acuteness of despair.

For us, time went pleasantly on and my turn came to go home on leave, and it was home for Christmas. We set out by truck on very icy roads, I recall, for Minden and caught a train for the Hook of Holland.

The crossing to Harwich was very calm, and anchor was dropped early morning and we lay to for some time. I reached home rather slowly – or was I impatient – and so to another happy reunion. It surprised me to see how much Jeff had grown and altered, it was the longest period we had been apart. Our conversation was very much concerned with when I should be demobbed. The groups at this moment being discharged were twenty-five or twenty-six, and we came to the conclusion that I should be home for June.

My wife, being the practical person she is, had let half of the house to a couple. She had, in fact, had several couples and been happy with them all, and during this leave I met her current tenants, Glenn and Irene. Glenn was an American soldier and he had married Irene, an English girl, not long before. Shortly after this they went to America. They still write every Christmas and we have seen them several times; the last time was 1978.

I was very depressed when this leave ended, it seemed so futile to go back for a few months, but mine was not to reason why. I must have always closed my mind on returning from leave because I can recall so little of return journeys.

There was very little to do in Bünde in our spare time during the winter; it was a one-horse town of meagre interest but our accommodation was reasonable and I recall we seemed to keep warm – having some good fires. There always seemed to be someone going home on discharge and small parties were arranged to bid them farewell.

Jimmy's discharge number was thirty-five and so he had to think of probably another six months in the forces after I left, but it didn't appear to concern him. He was now a sergeant so we saw less of each other of necessity; different ranks mixing socially have always been frowned upon which I suppose is quite logical.

The non-fraternisation rule was dropped but none of us had much to do with the locals. Germans cleaned the offices and living quarters and performed other similar duties. One such worker took my washing home to his mother for a ridiculously small charge – what they wanted was soap or cigarettes. He would take two shirts, underwear, socks and handkerchiefs and when I was giving him half a small tablet of soap he said 'Too much soap' – and then brought some back. On telling him to keep it he nearly cried. I never did understand the Germans and never experienced any rudeness or aggression. My experience is so different from all I have read both pre and post-war.

My wife and I often commented on this when we were on

holiday in Germany after the war. Another thing I noticed, when talking to Germans, they all declared they had fought on the Russian front, never against the British. The roads in Germany were very narrow and second class and no doubt Hitler improved transportation considerably with the autobahns.

The food situation was bad in Germany. The locals would hang around our dining halls, and as we left they would shout for *Brot*. On my leaving the country when I was on my final leave, I had, like others, a travel ration – and as the train pulled out of the station women were climbing up the railway embankment shouting for food. One woman with a child in her arms attracted my attention. I opened the carriage window and threw her a big sandwich but then some other person beat her to it. But as we all know today, the position is entirely reversed in Western Germany, no doubt due to their hard work and lack of strikes.

Entertainment for the forces was generally very good but, with such vast numbers of soldiers and airmen scattered through Europe and the East, events could not be expected very often. I saw and heard a number of good concerts, but where, I am now not quite sure. A good seat at the front was obtained for Yehudi Menuhin and I also saw *The Merchant of Venice*.

In addition to this sort of entertainment, towards the end of my service we had some very good discussion groups. On one occasion the lecturer was a private soldier who I understood was a PhD. The perfect instance of a square peg in a round hole. He had quite a debate with a Brigadier but, I must admit, it was well over my head.

Some of the people who came out from the UK, particularly from the Home Office, were a snooty lot. I never knew of any 'flare-ups' but there was no love lost between us. One day I said to our chief clerk, a sergeant, 'If I don't get out of here sarge, I shall go daft' – and off I went for a walk round Bünde.

My wife at this time had the problem of moving back to

Coventry. I had given my word that we would move out of the Nuneaton house on the owner's discharge from the forces. Eva and Jeff had been in this house on The Long Shoot since December 1940. We had a similar arrangement when we let our house, but they were able to get their own house repaired and return to it after I had joined the forces. Eva asked me if she should re-let it or return to Coventry. It was actually at the time flying bombs were dropping on London and, believing they could soon be aimed at Coventry, I advised Eva to re-let, which she did. She verbally arranged the same conditions. On her first application to get them out they refused, or made excuses. Eva had to seek a solicitor's help and he informed her she would have to share the house, and that is just what happened.

Chapter Fourteen

At long last notification was received of my demobilisation date. Vince Forte and I were going the same day, we said our farewells and were soon on our way.

By train we went to Tournai in France. I believe this is an old fortress town – I have read of it in the Marlborough wars. Remarks were going around that if one got through Tournai it was safe to assume your discharge was assured, but why, we never understood. It was with more than passing interest that we entered this old town. We entered a large camp and could see we were to be here some time; our papers were checked and we were interviewed and then we had to go through an Army Pay Corps office in a large tent to have our German marks exchanged into French francs. On producing the money I had to change, I also had to produce my army pay book. The clerk, having looked at this and the amount to be changed, referred me to a senior ranking officer to be questioned about having more cash than I had drawn over several weeks; nothing I said convinced them and about thirty pounds was taken from me. Vince lost more than I did and we felt very annoyed, it was then we recalled the remarks about getting through Tournai, people with very large amounts would probably be returned to face a court martial: some people, I understand, had been selling army equipment.

Vince had arranged to meet his girlfriend, so I wandered around and then lay in the sun. Later in the evening we had something to eat and then boarded the train for Calais. The set-up here was wonderful, it seemed everything was done for our comfort and happiness – a large camp with information offices giving everyone the chance to ask any questions relating to one's re-entry to Civvy Street. There was even a prefab house to show us what was being done to cope with the housing problem.

Arriving at Dover we had to go through the customs, but great reluctance was manifested by the troops in taking this step. It was quite funny; the officials were waiting for us and no one was going forward. It seemed quite ridiculous, so I stepped forward and slowly the others followed. When we were on the train a chap sitting next to me showed me a ladies' gold wristwatch in a box of matches. With a big wink he said, 'How's that'.

Flags were flying all along the railway from Dover to London; the roofs of houses were decorated and painted with big letters saying well done to the troops and airmen. This was evidently done when hostilities ceased, the south-east of the country would I suppose have more reason to demonstrate, having seen more aerial action and troop movement.

Paying some interest to where we were going and expecting to change trains in London, I was surprised to recognise places in the West End; we actually went quite close to Barons Court, where we were billeted prior to leaving London and so we made our way from the Southern Railway to the LMS. This was prior to the nationalisation of the railways.

We headed north and came to Manchester. Corporation buses conveyed us from the station to Ashton-under-Lyne, where a large cotton mill had been taken over to serve as a discharge centre. We parted with all we could such as army equipment, greatcoat etc, received our discharge papers and were then let loose to get civilian clothes of our choice, which were somewhat limited. We were then taken back to Manchester station. It was then I realised that I was out of the army; we could do what we liked, and we all made our own way home. With a ticket provided I was soon on a train for Coventry. Eva had now moved back to Sadler Road. I obtained a taxi at Coventry station, shared with an old neighbour of ours, and so got home at last.

It was very strange to tread on carpets again; it was something quite noticeable each time I got home, but this time I took my army boots off for good, had a bath and became a civilian again. The feeling was overwhelming and so it was to tell Jeff I was home for good, and to see the happiness on his face. The leave given was two months, I believe, which meant we had two months' pay but could start back to work whenever we chose. Eva had arranged a holiday at Felixstowe – at least I don't remember doing anything about it. Our Morris car had been laid up for the time I had been away and had come to no harm. Eva had it serviced prior to my getting home and so I was keen to get it on the road again. Quite a few people I knew who had had a car sold the vehicle on being called up and many regretted having done so. One colleague had a comparatively new 'Flying Standard Nine' which he sold in 1940, and on his return bought a car almost on its last legs, for double the amount he received for his previous car. No cars had been produced for private use throughout the war, hence the shortage.

We went on holiday to Felixstowe and enjoyed ourselves. I started to teach Eva to drive the car, but it proved to be more difficult than I imagined. Later we visited a number of friends and relatives and we were very pleased to visit Lichfield in comfort.

Jeff started at the local school and settled in quite well. For the two previous years or so he had been taught privately by a retired teacher at Nuneaton named Lucas, and this man would not take any payment for his efforts. Jeff loved him and he was a willing pupil. The Coventry school said he was well up to his age for learning.

Jeff tells me that I had six weeks before starting work. Our next happy trip was to visit Aunt Kit and Uncle Joe at their farm at Picklescott, which is in Shropshire, south-west of Shrewsbury. The farmhouse was half-timbered black and white, fifteenth century. I left the forces in late May and our holiday at the farm would be in July and we were right for the haymaking. Picklescott is about one thousand feet above sea level and the seasons are a little later. We had a very enjoyable week and the weather was very good. We helped

Uncle with the hay and many other jobs. Jeff was sure he only wanted to be a farmer – the two farm dogs would not leave him. To be alone with nature in the early morn on a bright day is pleasure indeed.

Uncle was very interested to hear where I had been on the continent. In 1914 Uncle Joe had been valet to Lord Brassey and when he rejoined the Life Guards, Uncle volunteered at the same time, and remained with him for the duration of the war. The laugh was that Uncle was only five feet eight inches tall but he still wore his Guards' tie.

Rabbits were still a popular dish with most ordinary folk and they were easily sold, because the meat ration was very small, but with the coming of myxamatosis in later years, the position was completely reversed. In 1946, though, I was able to borrow Uncle's gun and shoot a number of rabbits. Eva and Jeff loved fetching the cows up for milking and taking them back. The two dogs were so friendly and followed us everywhere we went, and when out shooting they were very obedient; they would set and then retrieve. One horse was kept on the farm, a big shire, her size being really remarkable: Jeff sitting on her back barely got his legs down the sides of 'Girlie'.

Picklescott was a very small village with fewer than twenty houses, no church, no school, and a small pub. One of Eva's aunts was staying at the farm when we got there, she was the widow of one of my father-in-law's brothers. There were six Brooks brothers and all were in the forces in the 1914 war. I only met three of them – Joseph, Harry and the youngest, Thomas, who is alive today and living in Richmond, Surrey – and is an extremely nice man who writes to us regularly.

I took Uncle Joe into Shrewsbury to the cattle auction and quite an experience that was – cattle get very wild in busy surroundings and farmers' talk is most intriguing. The week sped quickly by, we packed up and got the car in position to leave, but we could not find Jeff. We went into the barn and found him sitting on the straw with an arm round each dog's neck. He was quite unhappy to leave, but this was only one of many holidays on the farm. We called at Lichfield on our way home and found Mother and Father quite well.

I now had to think about work, and the Company were informed of my wish to start on a certain date. I was requested to attend Birmingham Divisional Office for an interview with the Divisional Manager. He was new to me and I didn't care for him very much and subsequently he retired early – but I cannot claim any merit for this. The people who achieved promotion and distinction in the forces, did not, it appeared to me, necessarily obtain any preference in our business when they returned.

One or two earned my disgust when they attended for their first interview dressed in officers' uniform. One that I saw at Birmingham, a naval officer, did get promotion and in his case it was deserved. I started back, working in two Birmingham districts and it felt most strange. The prospectus had been altered, as had the method of computation of premiums, so I was something of a stranger in a strange land.

On my way home one evening I called on Frank Redgrave, whom I had not seen since 1940. At the time I thought he had aged, but today, at seventy years, he only looks to be sixty. They had two dogs and wanted to part with one, a young spaniel, and offered to give it to me. I told them I would let Eva decide. Jeff was so keen I went back immediately and 'Soot' was a favoured member of our household for the next thirteen years.

After my first two or three weeks I was back working in my old districts of Leamington and Stratford. Norman Brown, the District Manager at the former, wrote me a delightful letter expressing his pleasure at my return.

Each agent I was with, whom I knew before the war, had much to talk about and we had many happy reunions. One I particularly remember was with an agent named Churchill. He lived in a village between Evesham and Stratford, and his house was in a field. He always took me home to lunch; his wife was a good cook and made me welcome. This agent was a great character and I always enjoyed his company – his main story will bear repeating. When he was called up, and after initial training, he found himself in the Royal Army Pay Corps working in Leicester.

He endured this office work for two years or more and then decided he had to get out, so he applied for a transfer and said he didn't mind where he went. He was subsequently posted and arrived at Bulford Camp where, to his great amazement, all the troops were wearing red berets – he had joined the paratroops. He completed his training and on D-Day his division was the first to land troops in France. They were dropped to take a river bridge a mile or two inland. Unfortunately he dropped wide of the desired spot. In the dark, and quite alone, he wandered about for some time and then a farmer took him in. The farmer sheltered him for a day or two because German troops were around. My friend said his biggest worry was the thought that he would be posted missing and his wife informed. Eventually British troops advanced and all was well. I heard many stories and escapades but will not bore you with any more. Shortage of petrol was still a big worry but we got by.

The problem at home was living in half a house and not having the use of my own garage. I went to the solicitor but all he suggested was selling the house to our tenants, he said we could get one thousand pounds, but I thought this a crazy idea. However, Mr Chetwood moved his job to Glasgow and after a while the family moved too, so we had the house to ourselves having shared for some nine months or so.

Our next item of interest was changing my job within the Company. Mr Wilby, of fire-fighting fame, and now back with the Company, came to see me one Saturday to tell me of a vacancy for Superintendent in Coventry West, my original district. At first I didn't feel too inclined, but my wife thought otherwise. I applied and got it and so my travelling days finished. The area I took charge of was the countryside of Coventry West, an area of about fifty square miles. Nearly all districts were still in the process of changing back from female wartime agents to men. Not all the men returned, for different reasons, and so we recruited new staff. This was not easy, with full employment being the order of the day. Sometimes we were lucky and got a good man but the modest salary and commission was not very attractive. To change agents meant a lot of work and long hours. An audit, which had to be taken in five days, meant working at great pressure and I did many sixteen-hour days. Coventry must have been one of the worst towns in the country to get staff for our business; with full employment and forty-hour weeks, the odds were against us. The comparison with districts outside the industrial areas was astonishing. The loss of staff, for instance, in Norfolk, Suffolk and similar places was mostly at normal retirement age, with replacements queuing up. In Coventry we nearly always had a vacancy.

There were only two long-established agents in my section, which meant I had to devote as much time as I could to selling to keep up my income. Mr Bridgstock, the man who started me, was still here at this time but he retired in 1950. We arranged a farewell dinner for him and it was one of the biggest of many such affairs I have attended. Officials from Birmingham office and many District Managers attended. The replacement was a man who seemed all bounce and little ability. We endured him for two years until he was moved to a London district.

It was becoming apparent that I should soon have to change my car after I had been back a year or more, but how to obtain one was quite a problem. Very few cars being built were coming on to the home market; they were all for export. Fortunately, Mr Nelms, a neighbour, put me in touch with a colleague at the Standard Motor Company who had a car only one year old which I bought for £450. The selling of my old Morris was quite amusing. Our local butcher put me in touch with a farmer very near to Edgehill. The farmer argued about price and asked me to take his two sons for a ride. They were big and heavy and suddenly I came to the famous hill and quickly had to get into bottom gear. The car made it and we arrived back for more bargaining. I was quite adamant and got my price of £275. When new in 1937 it cost £130 and I gave £75 pounds in 1938, so it can be seen inflation was with us in 1947 and has remained.

Chapter Fifteen

The 1944 Education Act was now in force and we were very interested in watching Jeff's progress towards his eleven plus examination. We went to his school to a parents' evening and had a very enlightening conversation with Jeff's teacher. I believed this teacher to be very competent – she told us she held a monthly test and the children were placed in the class according to their position in the test and Jeff was never out of the top few. In 1948 Jeff took his eleven-plus examination and also sat for the Bablake Governors' Scholarship. Bablake was well thought of as a Grammar and Headmasters' Conference School. For both examinations I took him in the car and met him afterwards; his remarks on meeting him I can still recall; they typify his modesty. Some time after these examinations we received a letter to take Jeff for an interview at Bablake School. The Headmaster at that time, Mr Seaborne, is still living I believe. He was a very big man and very strict and had no time for small talk.

He took Jeff into his study and I stayed outside. When Jeff came out, I had to go in, and the Head asked me if I was prepared to pay for my son to attend Bablake School, and I readily said yes. This to me was a stock question to see how keen I was to get him to this school. Within a couple of days, we received a letter telling us Jeff had obtained a Governors' free scholarship. This provoked memories of my first year in Coventry. When I was at Batts, my first job in Coventry, Mr Batt took me with him to this school, to measure certain boys for suits. Jeff having passed the Governors' exam was entitled to a new suit, providing the father's income did not exceed a certain figure, but my income exceeded this figure so excluded Jeff.

As mentioned, my new car was a Standard and we were very proud of it. Nearly all cars were still black but very soon the pastel shades became popular – indeed, this latest car was the last black car we had.

For holidays now we rented caravans; the reason for this was because Jeff was still having disturbed nights with coughing and caravans gave us a degree of privacy, but we still had one week on the farm each year. Over several years we had holidays at Beer, Paignton, New Milton and Littlehampton. At the latter place we called on Eva's cousin Edna Billingsley; she was one of Aunt Vin's daughters. This aunt lived near Kidderminister and was Uncle Joe's sister. Jeff enjoyed these holidays and so did we.

The transition to civilian life for me was happily accomplished, but certain aspects were very noticeable. For over four years I had done what I was told; personal endeavour was never very high on my chart of priorities in the army, but now if I wished to be successful and to attempt to tread the path of glory, then personal endeavour was paramount. It was at this time John Coltman and I resumed collaboration. He was the Ordinary Branch representative for Coventry and I had his services on my section for something like one day every two weeks. We enjoyed working together and wrote considerable business.

Nana Brooks, whom I have not mentioned since I returned from the army, had left her job and gone to nurse her sister, Aunt Pem, at Leicester. Alas, the illness proved fatal and she stayed on to look after her brother-in-law, Uncle Tom. After twelve months or so he found himself another wife and Nana Brooks went to live with Aunt Edie at King's Cliffe.

We were at this time most interested in seeing the first steps of Coventry's rebuilding programme. It was undoubtedly a major job and has since come in for both praise and criticism, but I think the authorities did quite well. It is so easy to be wise in retrospect. Many inconveniences had to be endured and makeshift shops at a certain spot one week would later be cleared away and one was left asking where Messrs so and so were now located. Our office was in Belvedere Road where it had been since the Hertford Street office had been destroyed. The district office had moved from Queen's Road to the centre of the city just prior to the start of the bombing. The Company had a very modern office built, but six months later it was in ruins and was never rebuilt. This meant that when I returned we had no claims office in Coventry and such matters were dealt with through Birmingham office. This arrangement continued until 1954. My friend Frank Redgrave was very active with his camera during this period and a year or so ago when we were spending an evening at his house he gave us a film show of Old Coventry and we found it most entertaining.

It is now thirty-five years since the war and my age is now seventy-three and I am still writing. The trouble is I get bored with the job and lay it aside for long periods. But now a capable young lady has started to type it I have regained my enthusiasm and am galloping on at an alarming rate.

Jeff started at his new school in September 1948. I went to his old school to express my thanks for their efforts. The headmaster was already known to me and he told me of the extent of their success. He said he had spoken to Mr Seaborne, headmaster of Bablake, who congratulated him on Hill Farm's vintage year, as he put it. I stayed chatting a short while when he asked me what I thought Jeff might become. I remember saying I hadn't the least idea, but he might become a teacher. The master looked at me in despair and said, 'never let him become a teacher – he will be a man among children and a child among men'. This remark surprised me and I have never forgotten it.

This was a very difficult period for Jeff and very worrying for us. He had a bad time with his chest, with bronchitis. He was ill and away from school for six weeks in his first term and seven weeks in the second term. Bablake had what I believe is known as the streaming system, with only the top stream taking Latin. Jeff started off in the top stream but at the end of the third term they asked him very gently to enter the second stream as it was impossible for him to keep up, with so much time away from school. This proved subsequently not to be a bad move because as he said himself he had a greater aptitude for science than for Latin.

I have often discussed with Jeff the ultimate success of the boys who went to this school with him in 1948. The first that springs to mind is Donald Trelford, the present editor of the *Observer* newspaper, who gained an open scholarship to Oxford University. Another friend of Jeff's later went to Birmingham University with him to become a doctor of medicine. My wife and I were extremely interested in our son's progress, and the reader who has laboriously stayed with me thus far will realise I was reliving my early years and enjoying with him what I foolishly cast aside in my youth. Such are the fond dreams of parents.

We attended Bill Talbot's wedding which was in 1950; he had been a boy when I took him and his mother from the bombing to Tamworth in 1940. I can always remember Bill's age because he was born in the same year as Granny Gilbert died, 1925, the latter being my wife's maternal grandmother; the bride being Joy Nixon. It was a happy occasion, but halfway through the wedding service Jeff fainted – I think the seriousness of the proceedings overcame him!

Bill Talbot came to Coventry with his parents in 1936, which I have already mentioned, and he certainly took advantage of the better educational facilities provided in this city. He started in the toolroom at the Alvis works and attended the Technical College for many years, obtaining his higher national certificate and progressing to C Eng, MIMechE, and became a Freeman of Coventry. He is at present in a good position with GEC at Rugby and Joy is music teacher at Leamington Kingsley High School. She plays the cello in the Warwickshire Orchestra and is a Licentiate of the Royal Academy of Music (LRAM). Very few people of my acquaintance have such a wide range of interests as Bill. He plays the violin, paints well, collects old books and makes string instruments. He told me last Christmas, when we spent a day with them, that he had been offered a very good price and pressed to sell a viola which he had completed recently. They are godparents to our grandsons, Peter and Alan.

Styvechale, a suburb on the south side of Coventry, is a very nice district and has a delightful church. Some of Jeff's school-friends came from this area and as a result he joined a youth club there and attended the church. This church was very small and was subsequently enlarged. The firm engaged to do this work was JR Deacon Limited of Lichfield, my brother's employers. My brother was apprenticed to another building firm in Lichfield to learn the joinery trade. His baptism into joinery, I understand, was hard and relentless. He absorbed what he was taught by a minor tyrant and subsequent employers recognised his worth. He made the oak doors at Styvechale church and I would like to think that Peter and Alan will one day inspect them. George spent most of his time in the workshop making woodwork for banks, churches and quite a lot for the extensions for Birmingham University.

George came to Styvechale one day to fit some work, and the vicar asked him if he would mind stopping work for a while, as he was about to hold a communion service. George, being a regular churchgoer, asked if he and his colleague could join the service. The parson was so delighted with this request he mentioned it in his sermon the following Sunday night.

My work at this time was very difficult, the staff problem being very trying and most annoying. The wages in industry were good and gave plenty of scope to write business as our premiums were most competitive. The bonuses added to policies were the best in the business, but our staff generally were not capable of taking advantage of the opportunities. My income was quite good but it could have been much better – it was made up of approximately sixty per cent salary and forty per cent commission. In Coventry we still had half our staff made up of wartime lady agents.

We found ourselves with a new District Manager who came to us from the adjoining district, a man very different from his predecessor. Mr Simpkin was a welcome change despite the fact that he and I had had a business argument some two years before. John Coltman left us, promoted to district manager at Malvern. John and Gwen invited us to tea one Sunday and we admired their new house very much. In John's place as OB representative we had Len Millen, an easygoing and humorous chap. We had an amusing experience one dark night when working together. We called on a farmer by appointment, and completed a sizeable contract. The farmer went upstairs for the first premium, paid in one-pound notes – this being quite common at this period from farmers who were selling eggs etc, on the side. I remember we had a drink and wished them goodnight. The last thing the farmer said was 'mind the duck-pond' and the next thing we heard was splash splash – Len Millen was in the pond. Back into the house we went. The farmer's wife produced clean socks and then Millen's humour took over and he had us all in stitches. As it happened, a medical examination was subsequently requested and the doctor turned our client down.

Changes in the fifties seemed to come frequently. Mr Simpkin left us after less than two years, when he was promoted to Divisional Manager. He went to the G Division which is in the north-east. The Company had the country divided into fourteen divisions, the Midlands being the H Division. In place of Mr Simpkin we had Mr Stan Karlson from Solihull. He was also a completely different type of man and at first was not very well liked. We had to explain to him that he was the fourth DM in four years and the staff were not happy with so many changes. He had a wonderfully keen brain and was well ahead in this respect. I often thought and compared my company and the army in their selection for promotion, and I am sure poor types are sometimes promoted in both cases. The people responsible, who decide on personal merit, are themselves lacking in many instances. This applies in all walks of life, I am sure. Who would say we have always had the best national leaders chosen from the many available?

While I was in the army a method of selection for officer training was started and from what I heard of it I approved, but it is probably always impossible to exclude some poor fish. My old friend Jimmy Brown went on one of those selections but was turned down. He told me he hesitated twice on an assault course and he thought that this counted against him, but I would think that from an intelligence angle he was well suited.

Our company after the war started something similar for promotions to District Manager. My friend Ernest Wilby, of fire-fighting fame, was chosen to go on a selection course but nothing came of it.

Chapter Sixteen

We had our first holiday on the continent in 1954. Eva was, and is, a great reader and longed to see a little of the countries she had read about. We discussed it at great length and I booked the Channel crossing through the AA. It was arranged that we make a leisurely trip to Switzerland.

We had just purchased a new Standard Eight car and felt well equipped for the journey. Although I had never driven on the right-hand side of the road, during the nearly two years I had been on the continent during the war I had seen and observed the differences in right-side travelling.

We thought it would be a good idea to call and see my cousin Len and his wife, Grace. We stayed with them on the Saturday night and were pleased to see them again. We had visited them once previously since the war but on that occasion had found our own accommodation to avoid troubling them. Their daughter, Audrey, was a very modern and sophisticated lass and Jeff liked her. In an earlier chapter I mentioned that Len, Grace and Audrey were at home when one of the first flying bombs dropped in the road outside their house, in 1944. The house completely collapsed and apart from an injured leg which Len suffered, they escaped, but, of course, were quite distressed. After it happened they could not find anywhere to stay. They eventually managed to get accommodation in Leicester. Grace was reduced to wearing odd shoes and it took days to get all the small particles of glass out of her hair.

When we arrived there in 1954 the house was, of course, completely restored and the garden was quite beautiful; the lawn looking like a billiard table. We had much to talk about and I recall next morning had a very leisurely breakfast with unfortunate results. Len showed us the road to go, he drove in front until we got to the Dover Road. I looked at my watch and found we had got an hour to catch the boat and, taking a few risks, went as fast as I could, but we missed it. The AA switched us to the Eastern Docks and put us on a boat for Dunkirk. This delay and a longer crossing meant we did not get far into France the first day. Our first night was spent in Hazebrouck, a well-known depot in the 1914/18 war.

Travelling on the right-hand side of the road did not inconvenience us: the front-seat passenger can be a big help when overtaking. I noticed the camber of the roads was very pronounced.

We found a reasonable place to stay the night and had a good meal of steak and chips. We set off next morning with the intention of making up for lost time. My wife and Jeff were quite thrilled to be in France and delighted to try and speak a little French.

We were making for Dijon, staying one night at Genlis. My wife always remembers this place because of the delicious soup we had, but I recall the small hotel because our French proved to be inadequate. Jeff came to our aid and explained what we wanted. I believe it was the third day that we reached Switzerland.

Our first view of the country was breathtaking. To view snowcapped mountains in the sun stretching as far as the eye could see was truly beautiful. We reached Geneva and found it even more interesting than we had envisaged. We stayed at Hotel Siècle and were well pleased; Eva found the shops quite staggering – in the prices they were charging as well as in their beauty. As I write these lines I am looking at the watch I bought in Geneva twenty-six years ago. One thing that this and subsequent holidays taught us was to enjoy continental breakfasts and we have made a habit of having rolls and coffee each Saturday and Sunday almost ever since. We visited Interlaken, Gstaad and a number of other places including the League of Nations offices. One small town we stopped at in France before we reached Switzerland was noticeable for the contrast between the high-quality hotel we stayed at and the apparent poverty of the town. Over the years, we saw how

France improved and in subsequent holidays often compared things to our first visit in 1954. The French people appeared very downcast at that time, they had not recovered from the war years which had been pretty awful for them.

We have turned up some of the receipts etc of this first continental holiday and the prices we paid for hotel accommodation seem today to be ridiculously low. On our way out of Switzerland, making our way towards Paris, we stopped at Berne and changed our Swiss francs into French currency and were pleased to make a little on the exchange deal. I liked motoring in France – the traffic in my time was fairly light with long stretches between villages but, oh! the pong in these villages.

It was noticeable in 1954 and for a year or two afterwards how British motorists waved to each other, but with the increased numbers journeying abroad, came nonchalance.

We continued our journey towards Paris but I cannot recall this part of our holiday in detail. Jeff was first to spot the Eiffel Tower on the horizon but the journey into Paris was a long one. We ran into more traffic than we had seen all the holiday. At this time there was a hooter silence in Paris but I forgot and hooted when the need arose, without any ill effect fortunately. To drive up the Champs Elysées is quite an experience; a dual carriageway with five lanes of traffic on each road. I can still recall feeling a little anxious going up this famous thoroughfare. We stayed at Hotel du Bois at 29 Avenue Victor Hugo. I had to turn left into this road but was in the wrong lane and got a little warm getting myself sorted out. This hotel was a bed and breakfast affair only and one eats in the French custom on the boulevards or as one wishes. There is so much to see in this beautiful city. We tried to see the main attractions such as the Sacré Coeur. Eva went on the Metro and Jeff and I walked to various places and saw Napoleon's tomb.

The next day we went to Versailles and saw the table on which the Peace Treaty was signed in 1919. This building is simply gigantic and beautiful; the approach is also very splendid. We stayed the night at a small hotel quite near and next day visited Fontainebleau and we were again staggered by the size and beauty of the palace.

Nothing that I can remember gave Eva more pleasure than this holiday and I knew it would be the first of many. We made our way back to Boulogne, or was it Calais? Eva and Jeff wandered around the boat while crossing the Channel but I always sat still as much as possible to avoid seasickness. We motored back home in good time, regretting the end of our holiday. As always after a break I returned to my job with some trepidation. Piles of post awaited me and it took two or three days to get my head above water. Important things would be dealt with by someone in my absence but anything that could be shelved was left, and the agents' problems would await my return.

Chapter Seventeen

1953 was the year that Jeff took his O level examinations and the results, as ever, were published during the summer holidays. The morning he went to the school to see the published results I arranged to stay in the office and I asked him to phone me. At Bablake School the students sitting the exam had to take the full range of subjects, not two or three one year and more the next. It was a proud day for me when Jeff rang and informed me that he had passed in all nine subjects that he had taken. He remained modestly calm and I think he would have been disturbed if he had failed one subject.

Coventry was still in an awful mess with all the rebuilding going on, the City Centre was being altered so much. Smithford Street was being closed, to be superseded by the Precinct. Broadgate was being realigned with the big store Owen Owen being moved and built over part of Cross Cheaping. It took more than twenty years to complete this building programme including the making of a new ring road. This new road has been a great boon, it being possible now to cross the town with a minimum of delay.

Many changes took place in our business and methods of remuneration were changed. The Approved Societies came to an end with the introduction of National Insurance, now renamed Department of Social Security.

Only two of my agents that I supervised in 1946 were with me when I retired. Mr Williams was one, and a more astonishing character it would be difficult to find. He was a good salesman but a wretched administrator – a man born to forswear orthodoxy but very likeable. He set his star to accumulate money and I must say he has succeeded. My association with him at times was very turbulent, but I readily admit my own income prospered by his efforts. Mr Coleman was the other agent; he was both a good salesman and a first-class administrator and as a consequence my life with him was happier. I have much to thank them for and do so. Had I had a few more agents of their kind I would be financially better off today. No further advancement came my way – production figures were the yardstick by which the company always measured one's progress and whilst I never expected further promotion, I never ceased to think the Company's method was wrong.

It must have been the following year that we went to Scotland. Eva had never been back to her place of birth but her mother had kept in touch with several of her friends. We first went to the Lake District and spent a night there and then travelled north-west over the Hardknot Pass to Cockermouth and then on to Carlisle where we stayed the night at, I believe, the Red Lion Hotel. From here we motored to Edinburgh and were delighted with the place. We booked in at a hotel off the north end of Princes Street and rang Ella Tait to let her know we were coming. She resided at Ogilvie Terrace but my pronunciation must have been adrift because each time I asked for this road no one had heard of it, but it came right in the end and we found Ella. She made a great fuss of us and could not do enough for Jeff. She could see a likeness between Jeff and Eva's father and she had very fond memories of the latter. She was a delightful person and later visited Coventry on two occasions. We visited Ella's sister and another friend, both of whom had lost their husbands in the 1914–18 war. The hospitality of the Scots is well known, but before the day was over we were feeling very uncomfortable, having had tea with Ella and then again at each of the other friends, followed by dinner at the hotel.

One visit I was looking forward to that same day was to see my army friend, Jimmy Brown, who lived at Gorebridge, a few miles outside Edinburgh. When Jimmy opened the door to us he was more than surprised but we were made most welcome and Mrs Brown was soon laying the table despite our desperate protests. She dished up sausages but how we managed to eat anything more was a mystery. We had much to talk about and thoroughly enjoyed the meeting before returning to our hotel, The Maitland, in the dark.

We left Edinburgh next day for Oban. It rained, I recall, and we were a little disappointed. We wanted to see the Highlands and pushed on north to Inveraray where we stayed the night and enjoyed the dinner of roast lamb and then went on to Fort William and Fort Augustus. Our journey along the banks of Loch Ness we much enjoyed. The weather picked up beautifully and so we came to Inverness. There we walked around but did not stay long, stopping that night at Grantown-on-Spey. Eva always recalls the open fires burning away.

We were keen to see the countryside around Balmoral so went on to Ballater. It was Sunday and we tried to get to Crathie church in time to see any Royalty going to morning service but we were too late. We were delayed by the single-line traffic, frequently having to pull in to cut-out spaces to let traffic go by. We saw the church and also the towers of Balmoral Castle. Later in the day, going through forest land, I had a flat tyre. It was quite a job changing the wheel because the car was on soft ground and the jack kept sinking in. Jeff was searching around for a flat stone but there appeared to be none around. We managed to change the wheel and I was then anxious to get the puncture mended.

We were to go many miles before I found a garage or an AA man. We cut across to the coast, but not for long as it was blowing cold, and then down to Perth, Stirling, Edinburgh through Durham and home. We stayed a night in the borders – the hotel was named The Black Dog. I mention this because we met an American couple staying there. They told us they had been travelling continuously for three months in Europe.

I now reach a period which was an unhappy one in family life. Nanna Brooks had moved from King's Cliffe, having bought a cottage at Enderby. This is a village on the Coventry side of Leicester. She was quite happy there living next door to Mrs Holt who was pre-war friend from Lichfield.

We had been to the farm at Picklescott each year and Jeff and his schoolfriend Bob Allen had also had a holiday at the farm. Uncle Joe was going downhill, however, in the early 1950s, and he had to sell the farm. Before doing so he had a bungalow built in a field he owned, opposite the farm. We spent a holiday here, but it was not long before Uncle was in Shrewsbury hospital where he died in November 1955. My father had been unwell for some time and alas, in January 1956, he passed away – and an uncle and aunt also died at Whittington. With so many ageing relatives we had to accept this sad recurring experience.

Aunt Kit came to see us and expressed a wish to live nearer to us; she thought it would be a good idea if Eva's mother and she bought a house and lived together. Eva and I had misgivings about this but went along with the idea. The house they bought was in Browns Lane, in Coventry, and it cost £2,200. Jeff and I attended to the garden and we thought things were going along quite nicely, but friction was slowly developing. It was fifteen months after losing my father that we suffered the sad loss of my mother: it was a very painful period. About eighteen months later Aunt Kit left and she bought a house just outside Blackpool. She was influenced by a friend we know. Despite this we did not feel that Kit had been too unreasonable – Eva's mother was not easy to live with.

Jeff was now taking his A level exams; he passed in all three subjects, maths, physics and chemistry. He made applications for a university place stating first choice as Birmingham. I can clearly recall the morning he went for his interview. He wondered what they were likely to ask him. Quite fortunately I gave him good advice. I suggested they would probably ask why he had chosen Birmingham University and also which daily paper he read. They asked these very questions and also what the editorial column was discussing that morning. They accepted him, but deferred his entry for a year because of his age. He was now a school prefect and school life was happy, and so it continued – so much so that he was loath to leave when the time came. He took the A level exams again the following year with good results getting a distinction for maths and physics.

Jeff had taken up tennis and badminton and over the years has had lots of pleasure from these games. I asked him to give me a game of tennis one weekend and we played on a hard court in the Memorial Park, and I put everything into the game. Who won is quite forgotten but I lay exhausted the whole of the next day, Sunday, and have never played since! My last game prior to this was the day the IRA bomb exploded in Broadgate, Coventry, in 1939 which I missed by some two hundred yards or so, the explosion killing five people.

I would like very much to let my grandchildren know something of our continental holidays but I do not want them to think our life was all holidays; it was much the reverse. Before the war we had two weeks' holiday each year, which soon after became three weeks and latterly, four.

My wife got tired staying at home so much and got herself a job soon after I got back from the forces. Jeff at that time had a bad spell of health and she had to give up after a few months. Two or three years later she found another job and worked for seven years approximately but only part-time. This work gave her a greater interest and additional income was welcome.

Friends of ours, Ken and Ave Green, were very keen travellers on the continent and asked us to go with them. I think our first holiday with them would have been 1955. Ken drove his sister Dora's car, a Vauxhall Cresta. There were four of them with Dora and Ken's daughter Wendy, who was a little younger than Jeff. We went abroad with them several times during the 1950s and we always planned our route but did not always keep closely together; sometimes I would lead and sometimes Ken.

At this distance of time it is a little difficult to separate the holidays; the first one certainly took us to Vienna. This was a long journey and Austria had only recently been freed, the

Russians having given up their part of the country. It was very good weather and on the second day Ken asked me if I would like to change cars. It was quite enjoyable to drive the Vauxhall with its much greater power. The road for many miles before reaching Vienna is very straight, through wooded country. Our stay in Vienna was for a day or two only but we saw as much as possible in that time. We obtained accommodation at a fairly good hotel and found this city most interesting.

The line of division between the Russian and British and American sectors was very noticeable. We travelled by tram into the former Russian area and found it very dirty and uncared for. We saw the Danube but found it very unlike our romantic image of it. While in this town I found myself seeking traces of its legendary past, and the dimly lighted cafes and Viennese music recalled the Strauss family and in a beer garden we seemed to step into the nineteenth century.

We returned home quite determined to see more of the continent in future years and our next holiday with the Greens was southern France and northern Italy. We lingered in Monaco viewing the famous or infamous casino and the Palace. We have a snap of Ken drinking local beer from a litre glass, sitting on the Palace wall. While we were here we saw the Onassis yacht, the *Christina*, in the harbour. This is undoubtedly a very beautiful place and to travel as we did, via the Corniche roads into Italy, and seeing bougainvillaea, oleander and tamarisk all in bloom is something to remember; the cypress trees growing in Italy always seemed to me more attractive than elsewhere. On our way, going uphill out of Monaco, I noticed that liquid was pouring from Ken's car. It was difficult to overtake on this road but we got them to stop and discovered a water container had overturned. I remember we stopped in Menton to dry Ken's car boot and contents.

Ken Green was a colleague, with the same position with the Company as myself, and was a very intelligent chap – his historical knowledge of the many places we passed through was quite extraordinary; Jeff and I had some interesting conversations with him.

Another year we were with Ken and family and went over a number of Austrian passes, the Gross Glockner being the highest. Looking back to these climbs over mountain passes, I now get a little perturbed that I ever dared to drive in such hazardous terrain. We were proceeding through the Alps on one occasion when Ken stopped to tell me his brakes had failed and he wanted our wives to change cars for some reason which I have quite forgotten. The place I recall perfectly was north of Heiligenblut and I was feeling at the time a little apprehensive but Eva was quite blasé and we reached Heiligenblut without mishap.

Moving on into Italy I made a mental note of the mileometer at a certain point and found on our arrival at Merano, we had covered twenty miles without touching the accelerator; it had been downhill all the way. Narcissi were growing in profusion for miles on the mountainsides and with them we saw edelweiss. Merano is very beautiful and my wife believes it to be her favourite town with its natural layout being very attractive. On our first visit to this lovely spot we had breakfast on the balcony of the hotel. This place attracted us so much that Eva and I went back to it for a holiday some years later, but without the car. When we were touring Austria with the Greens one year it was the bicentenary of Mozart's birth and Salzburg, his birthplace, was crowded when we arrived there, so we viewed his house on a later occasion. However, we tried every hotel we could find, but could not get rooms, so we indulged in a very good dinner and then asked the police if they could find us some accommodation. Their only suggestion was the police cells so we had to stay in the cars.

We discussed where to park for the night and I suggested staying within the town but I was outvoted and we moved off into the country. We stopped in a hilly and wooded part, and locked ourselves in – but to try and sleep comfortably in a car is almost impossible. I felt a little apprehensive of our position because a year or so before this we had read of British travellers being murdered in their cars in France.

I could not get to sleep and after some two hours or so I

was startled, but kept quiet, when I saw a man in the trees walking aimlessly along. However, he passed by and the dawn eventually broke with nothing to report, and a very beautiful dawn it was. In the daylight we saw we had stopped at the foot of a pass and the figure I had seen in the night had been near to a farm we could now see. We soon drove to the top of the pass where we found Ken washing his face at a mountain stream and shouting to us *trinkenwasser*. These were certainly very happy holidays.

Chapter Eighteen

My work was keeping me fairly occupied but business was good and we were saving money on a regular basis. My wife and I have always been completely frank in money matters; she is such a wonderful manager, I have no inhibitions. I have seen too many husbands pass on, leaving wives short of money, and of money sense.

When Jeff sat his intermediate exams he was somewhat perturbed and thought that he had muffed it, but he passed alright and then went on to his finals. I always had complete faith in him and my attitude was justified when he obtained his BSc with honours. But looking back over the years, I think I have been too critical of him to his face but very ready to sing his praises to the world, but again I am also self-critical as, indeed, Jeff is.

Sometime before Jeff left university we moved house. We had always liked Allesley Village, which had been taken into the City boundary in the 1920s, and the house we bought was near the centre of the village. That is now twenty-two years ago and property has increased ridiculously. We gave £2,650 and now in 1980 I understand it would sell for over £30,000. We were very happy with our new house and over the years have a number of improvements made.

Having completed his education, Jeff, during the first week he was at home, said how strange it was to have no commitments – no studying and time to spare. He had had several interviews with potential employers and, from these, follow-up interviews at the different works. He went to British Nuclear Power, and to Courtaulds, but the others I have forgotten. He chose Courtaulds and I believe never regretted the choice. We pulled his leg and told him it was mother's cooking, as he would be living at home initially. Since then he has had promotions and remains happy with the Courtaulds Group.

It was about this time that Jeff got interested in tracing our family tree. He first went to the local library and obtained a book on the subject which we read with great interest. He decided we ought to get in touch with my late father's only surviving brother, Uncle Fred. To do this we wrote to the War Office, because we had no idea where he lived or, indeed, if he was still alive. They replied, stating that if a letter were written, it would be forwarded. Jeff wrote, and in the letter said he hoped that he was writing to his grandfather's brother.

Uncle wrote a very nice letter back stating he was the relation in question. He asked after all the family and invited us to visit them in Bournemouth, to which Jeff replied and our visit was arranged. I had last seen Uncle in 1934, and Aunt Amy in 1923. We paid our visit on a Sunday and I recognised them immediately. We had much to talk about. They did not know that my mother and father had passed away. Uncle regretted that they had lost touch with my father but he said he had written to him from Cairo, after he had rejoined the army, having retired just prior to the war. I told him Father had not heard from him since they had last met in 1940 at their father's funeral.

Uncle had retired as a Lt Col: I told him I had been in the army but did not inform him of my rank! We looked at lots of photographs, including Dennis and his wife and three sons. Dennis had obtained the MC at Dunkirk and we learned that his wife had died some years later, from polio. The youngest boy had been adopted by Frieda, Dennis' sister. They then told us that Dennis had resigned his commission in the army and had acquired a publishing business in London. He had also married again, someone from the Guinness family, but whether a close or distant member of the brewing family I never discovered.

I stated earlier that Frieda had married a second cousin, Arthur Snelling, having been at University with him. He subsequently went into the Diplomatic Service and we were shown photographs of Frieda in different parts of the world. At one time he was British High Commissioner in Ghana and for his services was awarded the KCMG, KCVO, and so they became Sir Arthur and Lady Wendell Snelling. Aunt Amy and Uncle Fred were very modest about the achievements of their son and daughter – Uncle was much more interested to ask Jeff what degree he had obtained and what work he was doing. We had tea with them and enjoyed our visit. We never saw Uncle again; sadly he died some short time after this visit. My aunt wrote to us once or twice and we visited her when she moved into a flat in Bournemouth. I believe Frieda and her husband are now living in retirement in Richmond. We did not get much family history from Uncle and that which he gave us was subsequently proved to be inaccurate. We informed cousin Len and Grace of our visit and they, I believe, also contacted them. They had been in touch during the early part of the war when they had been living not too far apart in Surrey.

Jeff enlisted cousin Audrey's help in his efforts to compile a family tree. Audrey was a secretary in the West End and she and Jeff frequently corresponded. When visiting Len and Grace we took the opportunity of inspecting relevant church records and useful information was obtained from churches in Kent. Audrey and Jeff were a good team and their tenacity of purpose paid off, and so, after months of diligent effort, they traced the Barnes line back to about 1720.

My brother lost his wife in 1965. Coming after losing our parents, George saw more of that sad period than I did, as he still lived in Lichfield, and went through a very traumatic time.

In 1966 Audrey was married to Peter Scott, a medical doctor. We were invited and took George with us. At that time they were still living at Beddington. For a time Peter was in practice in London but he transferred his activities to Thorpe Bay in Essex. Len and Grace moved there too, and were much in demand as babysitters.

On my father's side I suppose we have not been a close family as the following will show. My brother received a letter some time after he had lost his wife, from a firm of family researchers in London, asking if he was the son of Joseph McLinden Barnes. George gave me the letter and asked me to reply to it. The letter informed us that an Edward John Drake had died in 1968, intestate and unmarried. I replied giving them all the information I could concerning our family. They were pleased with the information and promptly thanked me and informed me that Lloyds Bank Ltd, Croydon Branch, were dealing with the estate and were the Executors. I asked the bank the extent of the estate and where the money was invested. The information I received was that the total value of the estate left was some £15,000 and the money was in two Building Societies.

My father's mother's maiden name was Drake and the deceased Edward John was therefore my father's cousin. It took a further two years before the estate was cleared, a total of six years. I wrote and received letters about the estate and learned the truth of the adage: 'Legal lucidity, unlike literary simplicity, is often attainable only through a mass of verbiage.' The money left increased by interest to £19,000 but the total number of relatives traced, who were also beneficiaries, was sixty-five, my share being £313.

In 1960 my District Manager was ill and I took his place for a month or two. I still had my own section to manage plus the responsibility for the district, a staff of about twenty-five and a district office. Mr Karlson had had a coronary and I believe was away for about twelve weeks. During this time the staff supported me very well and we maintained good progress.

Since I retired I have realised what time and effort I put into my job and now know that many people took an easier course with no less material benefits, but undoubtedly gained in other ways. A year or two later Eva and I were on holiday in the south coast where we had been along to Brighton to see Vince Forte. Eva looked round the shops and I made my way back to the car because I felt ill. My wife knew nothing of this until we got home. The result subsequently

Eva and Bill in 1960

was I was put in hospital for a fortnight and later informed I had suffered a coronary and was now an angina subject. This disturbed me quite a bit at the time but I have learned to live with it, and have since enjoyed life very much. I was now within a few years of my retirement and was looking forward to it. I have never been able to understand people who dread retirement – getting old is not pleasant but to have time to do the personal things one is interested in, is surely desirable after years of effort.

The Company informed me that I could continue beyond my sixtieth birthday if I wished, and I gave this some thought. An interesting matter occurred about this time – our staff union were pressing for a revision of the staff pension. Our pension was based on the retiring age of sixty years and was sixty per cent of average last three years of salary. However, all the field staff also received commission and an annual bonus, but this was ignored for pension computation. The union were pressing for this commission to be included, and being very significant, I was anxious to know what was to be the outcome. The Company agreed that earnings other than salary should be included for pension on a sliding basis for the next eight years, in the following manner. Average commission and bonus earnings over the last ten years of service would be dealt with as for salary but discounted by forty per cent for the first year and then reducing by five per cent per annum.

This commenced one year before I retired and I was able to assess my subsequent pension. It would be three-fifths of my retiring salary and sixty-five per cent of sixty per cent of my average commission earnings over the past ten years. This was quite acceptable and I retired six months after my sixtieth birthday, in July 1968.

My wife and I were invited to Chief Office and taken out to lunch. In Chief Office I was received by one or two head people and it was all very pleasant. We stayed that night at the Regent Palace Hotel and saw the long-running play *The Mousetrap* by Agatha Christie.

The Company paid all expenses and we returned home having very much enjoyed ourselves. London is certainly a wonderful place, although we go there seldom nowadays.

Chapter Nineteen

Jeff enjoyed his sporting activities and occasionally called in home with a girlfriend but my wife and I believed he would be a long time choosing a partner and so it proved. However, by the late 1960s Jeff was playing a lot of badminton and mentioned a young lady named Pat whom he often partnered in matches, and one evening he called in home with her – but whether or not this was to be a lasting affair or a casual one we had no idea.

Soon after this Jeff was promoted to Laboratory Manager at Derby. He had commenced at Courtaulds in 1959 and had been Head of the Textile Section in a Coventry laboratory for the previous three or four years. He found a lot of work at the new laboratory and much reorganisation was required, but I believe he enjoyed the challenge. He stayed in Derby two or three nights each week at accommodation provided by the Company. I recall him telling me that he was happy with the responsibility of management. Some eighteen months later Pat and Jeff became engaged and Eva and I were quite delighted. We met Patricia's mother and father and celebrated the occasion by having dinner out.

Unfortunately the increase in house prices took off at this time and so made the search for a house more difficult. They searched continuoually over a long period and also over a wide area. They settled for a house to be built at Dunstall, near Burton, but the builder let them down badly and that came to nothing. Jeff, getting married at a later age than most people, had one compensating factor: he had saved rather more money and this was very fortunate in view of house prices. He insisted on living in the country and would not consider the town.

When Jeff started work he had also enquired about evening teaching at the Technical College, and they took him on and he taught maths for one or two nights a week for a few years. This enabled him to buy his first car, as he would not accept any help from us, and we naturally admired his independent attitude. About 1969 he became an Associate Member of the Textile Institute so we wagged our tails a bit more. We were seeing a lot of Pat now and the more we saw the more we liked her. She is a most admirable girl and she and my wife are bosom pals. All the good traits my wife has, Pat has too.

Eventually Jeff and Pat found a suitable property, but the price shook me at the time. Today, eight years later, it is quite a normal price. Some alterations were carried out, such as changing grates and enlarging the kitchen, and it is now a most desirable residence. Friends of my brother carried out these alterations.

The work that was done by the family, apart from the builders, was quite amazing and I would say was a source of enjoyment for one and all. Our contribution, that is my wife and I, with George and his neighbour Ann, was quite considerable. We would meet at the house and start a pre-ordained task, have a pleasant lunch and work on till evening. It became one of my tasks to get the lawns into good order – there was, and still is, a lot of grass cutting at Downend. The combined efforts, which included Jeff and Pat, and Pat's parents, meant that much of the interior of the house was redecorated before they moved in. This house is in Derbyshire, but the nearest town, Ashby, is in Leicestershire and Burton-on-Trent, only eight miles away, is in Staffordshire so the postal address of the house, Boundary, is very apt.

Pat and Jeff were married on the 29th September, 1973 at Allesley Church and reception at the new Post House Hotel. The usual gathering of relations and old friends took place and it was a very happy occasion.

Pat was a civil servant, working in several different branches of the service, at one time with the Post Office. At the time of their marriage she was working at the Naval Depot in Coventry; this was somewhat secret work and she never discussed it. She had to go down to Portsmouth a few months before they were wed, I believe this was to sort out stock. She did not go to university, but she could have done and Jeff is certain she could have got a good degree.

On moving to Derbyshire Pat could not obtain work in the service locally and, being keen to work for a while, she obtained a job in a small engineering works. Pat has two married sisters, one living in Nottingham and the other at Knutsford.

Uncle Arthur and Aunt Nell had been looking forward to Pat and Jeff's wedding but unfortunately Aunt Nell died a while before.

Our longed-for first grandchild arrived some eighteen months later on the 27th March, 1975 and was named Peter William, and, of course, we could not see enough of him – our cup of happiness was full. We stayed with Jeff while Pat was in hospital and then Pat's mother took over for a week or so.

Much has been written and spoken of grandparents spoiling grandchildren but we have not been guilty in this respect, despite the fact we literally live for them. Alan Jeffery was born on 21st September, 1977. Now that they are growing up they come and stay with us and Nana and Grandpa are as proud as peacocks. When Alan was with us recently at about age three and a half, I asked him 'If he had two apples and I gave him another two, how many would he then have?' He promptly replied, 'too many'.

When I last mentioned Audrey and Peter Scott they were living in Thorpe Bay where we visited them several times. They moved to Bristol two or three years ago and cousin Len and Grace moved there also and the latter celebrated their Golden Wedding in 1979. We were invited together with Pat and Jeff and George also. We had lunch at the Ashton Court and Country Club Hotel. Peter is now Chief Medical Officer to a company in Bristol. Audrey and Peter have three fine boys and, with Jeff, keeping up the remarkable succession of boys in the family, Audrey herself was only the third girl since 1850. When we go to the West Country, which is almost every year now, we call and see them.

I fondly imagined that when I retired incomes would remain fairly stable, a desirable thought when in receipt of a fixed income, but the reverse has been the experience. Inflation has always existed but never has it been so rapid as during the last ten years. My Company have been very good and increased pensions every year, but not sufficient to combat inflation; our modest invested capital is very comforting.

Eva and I continue to enjoy our holidays which we take most years. I avoided flying for so long – yes, I know I am not one of the bravest – but I agreed to fly to Italy in 1970 and found it both enjoyable and fascinating. We stayed near Lake Como, but the heat was very trying at Tremezzo where we were staying. This had been the place where Mussolini, the Italian dictator, had finally been shot. The food in Italy does not appeal to me nearly so much as in Germany and Austria, but I suppose their prowess in the culinary art is no less.

Continuing my thoughts and observations on the subject of inflation, one is continually speculating on the future. The political situation at the moment is very vexed and is a repetition of my youth, with an unemployed total approaching three million.

Successive governments have avoided facing up to the cold fact that we do not pay our way, but the present government is becoming very unpopular by their efforts to do the right thing. I am as true a blue as ever, and I am sure they must pursue the present course, despite the misery of high unemployment. The Labour Party at present is in an awful mess; they have so many neo-communists in their ranks, a position that has grown steadily worse since Lord Attlee's time, and now is splitting asunder with a number of right-wing socialists breaking away to form the new Social Democratic Party with the Liberals. I have a feeling this new party will do well and the demise of the Labour Party, as we know it, will come about.

My wife and I frequently discuss the current political and

A family group, 1991 (standing) Jeff; (sitting) Peter, Alan, Bill, Eva and Pat

economic situation, particularly with reference to the grandchildren. As I see things, a good education is more necessary than ever and I still recall with what envy I looked at young chaps who were articled to a profession and my two choices would still be chartered accountancy or law.

It still appears to me that we have been singularly fortunate to have achieved whatever little we have with so little formal education.

It would be appropriate I feel for Peter and Alan to know that Aunt Kit and Nanna Brooks both left money to us which we have invested together with our own savings. We fondly hope we can leave Peter and Alan something which they will one day appreciate. Looking back, as we do, and knowing their early history and their trials and troubles, we find it quite remarkable that Nanna Brooks and Aunt Kit managed to accumulate any money and still maintain a respectability which was quite outstanding. Our forebears have certainly impressed and influenced Eva and me. The sixty-four thousand dollar question is, shall we influence our successors – or is it even pertinent to expect such influence? An outsider reading this may assume that we feel ourselves as custodians for the money left to us, but such attitudes can become illogical with the passage of time. I must abstain from influencing the ones to inherit, and merely say that there is no greater factor than common sense, a quality I am sure my descendants have in plenty.

Well, I started out with some trepidation to write for you, Peter and Alan, but now my mission is accomplished.

Our daughter-in-law, Pat, wrote in her inimitable old English writing, as a present for me that I still treasure, Gray's Elegy, and so I end with these famous lines:

> The boast of heraldry, the pomp of pow'r,
> And all that beauty, all that wealth e'er gave,
> Awaits alike th' inevitable hour,
> The paths of glory lead but to the grave.